Women Around

This script is published by
DCG Publications.

All inquiries regarding purchase of further scripts and current royalty rates should be addressed to:

DCG Media Group
Vamos 73008
Chania
Crete
Greece

Email: info@dcgmediagroup.com
www.dcgmediagroup.com

Conditions

❖ All DCG Publication scripts are fully protected by the copyright acts. Under no circumstances must they be reproduced by photo-copying or any other means, either in whole or in part.

❖ The license to perform referred to above only relates to live performances of this script. A separate license is required for video-taping or sound recording, which will be issued on receipt of the appropriate fee.

❖ The name of the author shall be clearly stated on all publicity, programs etc. The program credits shall state "Script provided by DCG Publications".

Women Around

By

Glyn Jones

DCG
Publications

First Published in Greece 2010

© Glyn Jones

The author's moral rights have been asserted

DCG Publications
www.dcgmediagroup.com

ISBN 978-960-99470-1-5

Typeset by
DCG Publications

Printed in England by
Lightning Source.

First Produced
at the

Connaught Theatre,
Worthing

February 16th - 27th 1971

Directed by
Glyn Jones

Lighting	Set design
David St John	Hans Christian

Assistant to the Director
Christopher Beeching

Cast List

Alma	Joyce Heron
Crispin	Adrian Wright
Dolores	Betty Alberge
Charlotte	Caroline Dowdeswell
Fanny	April Walker
Angela	Zienia Merton
Jason	Errol Bolger

Time: 1970's

Women Around - Set Design Hans Christian

Act One

The time is 1970 – the room is fifty years before. Fifty years of turbulent history has sent the world screaming into the space age and has left the room untouched. It is a first floor drawing room and, from its shape, one would suppose the house to be Georgian in Chelsea. The room is at once rich but colourless, opulent, sumptuous, drab and shabby. If you look closely at the fine china you will see the nicks and cracks of time, the missing fingers, the petals snapped off tiny flowers. You will find the marble of the huge fireplace stained and pitted, the brocade of the chairs grubbied from years of hands, elbows and the backs of heads. The craftsman made, lovingly put together tables are loosening at the joints, chipped veneer leaving jagged scars. The gilding on heavy picture frames is beginning to peel, and the silver backs of fine bevelled mirrors to blister. But, whatever else the room might breathe, the sighs of old ghosts, the musty stillness of dead years, the stale smell of powder and perfume the occupants no longer notice, it also breathes an unchanging essence of security in a rapidly changing world.

Large French windows, framed in heavy, dust gathering drapes, lead to a narrow, completely useless balcony which overlooks a small walled garden below. Could there really be hollyhocks growing by the wall?

Double doors lead into the room.

It is late afternoon. The windows are wide open but, although bright outside, this room never has the brightness of sunlight. In a huge, comfortable old sofa in front of the fireplace a woman in negligee is seated, a very beautiful woman who has kept her looks and figure into middle age and so looks much younger than she actually is. She stares dreamily into the fireplace, softly stroking the head nestling in her lap; a delicate, elegant head.

The woman is ALMA. The boy is CRISPIN. He lies on the sofa with his back to the fire, his knees pulled up to touch her side. He is wearing a short, highly coloured bathrobe and when he suddenly stretches it is like a cat right down to his toes. Relaxing from the stretch he reaches over his head and gropes for a silver sweetmeat dish standing on a piecrust table beside the sofa. ALMA laughs and reaches out for him.

ALMA: And what is my darling looking for?

CRISPIN: You don't know?

ALMA: Crème de menthe.

CRISPIN: Huh-huh.

ALMA: *(Fiddling with the sweets)* What would you say... If I were to say... there's no crème de menthe?

CRISPIN: I would pack my bags and leave.

ALMA: Would you really? Why don't we both?

CRISPIN: What?

ALMA: Pack up our bags and leave.

CRISPIN: Just the two of us?

ALMA: Hmn-Hmn.

CRISPIN: I don't know. Where would we go?

ALMA: How about... Fiji?

CRISPIN: *(Giggling)* Why Fiji?

ALMA: First place that came into my head.

CRISPIN: All right, we'll go to Fiji. But first, let's eat. Yarrakooroo mongy mongy. That means, Fiji warrior, him very hungry.

ALMA: Hungry for what, my darling?

CRISPIN: Sweet things.

He turns his back and opens his mouth wide. She holds the piece of crème de menthe over his open mouth. He stretches his neck, reaching up with his head. She pulls the sweet away a little, waves it under his nose.

Come on, come on.

She laughs and teases him a moment longer.

ALMA: What a pink tongue you have.

CRISPIN: What colour did you expect it to be?

He stretches out his tongue, reaching for the titbit. She drops it into his mouth. As he bites into it he groans and squirms with pleasure, stretching his toes, curling them, stretching again. She laughs.

ALMA: What pretty feet you have.

He lifts his head to look at them and wiggles his toes.

CRISPIN: Hmn... they are rather, aren't they? *(He drops his head back on her lap)* They're a gift of nature.

ALMA: What?

CRISPIN: Pretty feet. That's what Goethe said. Pretty feet are a gift of nature he said. When I'm dead... they will be a lot of little white bones. Little white spiky bones.

She laughs and strokes his face. He kisses the palm of her hand.

ALMA: Isn't it time you put on some clothes?

CRISPIN: Is it? Why?

She shrugs.

> Don't you like me as I am?

He opens his mouth again. She searches the dish for the crème de menthe and holds it over his mouth.

ALMA: Say please.

CRISPIN: Please.

She pops the sweet in his mouth and his teeth close over her fingers. She squeals as he growls and worries the finger. He releases it and she examines it for teeth marks.

> That's for making me say please.

ALMA: Little boys should always say please. Little boys should remember their manners. Sweets are bad for you. They'll spoil your complexion.

CRISPIN: Why do you keep them so handy then?

ALMA: They'll make you fat.

CRISPIN: Right in temptations way.

ALMA: To spoil you.

CRISPIN: Of course. *(He inspects her finger)* Did I hurt you?

ALMA: Did you want to?

CRISPIN: Kiss it better. *(He does so)*

ALMA: You should be spanked.

Obligingly he turns over on his stomach. She pulls up the dressing gown to reveal him naked underneath and slaps his buttock, her hand lingering a fraction longer than it should. She gives him a look and, as he hasn't reacted, slaps him again, a little harder. Still no reaction. She gives him a resounding slap. There is a yell, a flurry of bathrobe and naked flesh, and in a moment, he is three yards from the sofa, facing her and rubbing his backside.

CRISPIN: You didn't have to do that.

She is laughing again and holds out her hand to get him back.

ALMA: Come here.

CRISPIN: No.

ALMA: Come here. *(Nothing. She drops her hand)* All right, don't come here.

She looks away towards the fire place. He hesitates a second and then moves to the front of the sofa where he kneels beside her. She strokes his head.

You know your trouble don't you? You were brought into the world spoilt.

CRISPIN: Shamelessly.

ALMA: Such conceit.

CRISPIN: Why do you stare into an empty grate? You can't make dreams out of a cold empty grate.

ALMA: You can make dreams out of anything.

CRISPIN: Bad dreams.

ALMA: You don't have bad dreams. You never had a bad dream in your whole life.

CRISPIN: I did too.

She waits.

When father died.

The woman stiffens perceptibly. The hand stops moving.

　　　　　　　　　　Don't you have any work to do?

ALMA:　　　　　　Are you trying to get rid of me?

CRISPIN:　　　　　No. *(Pause, then absently)* Not particularly.

ALMA:　　　　　　I suppose we ought to.

CRISPIN:　　　　　What?

ALMA:　　　　　　Move.

CRISPIN:　　　　　Hmn… *(He snuggles down more comfortably.)*

ALMA:　　　　　　Why don't you go and sit with your grandmother for a while? Before supper. She would like that.

CRISPIN:　　　　　Trying to get rid of me?

ALMA:　　　　　　I might think about it. If you're not very very good.

She puts her hand on his chest inside the dressing gown. He immediately gets to his feet and heads for the door.

　　　　　　　　　　Where are you going?

CRISPIN:　　　　　I don't know. To put some clothes on.

ALMA:　　　　　　You aren't thinking of going out.

CRISPIN:　　　　　Hmn?

ALMA:　　　　　　Are you going out?

CRISPIN:　　　　　I don't know. I don't think so.

He steps towards the door just as it opens and DOLORES enters using the upstage of the two doors. Although older by only a year or two than her sister, DOLORES has not worn nearly so well. Perhaps because she is very thin, perhaps because she is a spinster and a certain bitterness has etched its lines in her face. She is neatly dressed, clothes for the office, and carries paper parcels as well as the usual handbag, umbrella, gloves. CRISPIN stands looking at her. ALMA doesn't move. She is staring again into the fire. DOLORES looks from one to the other.

DOLORES: What a cosy little domestic scene.

ALMA: Is there any reason why it shouldn't be?

DOLORES: Well, I'm sure we have better things to do with ourselves than sit around all-day in the next to nothing.

ALMA: Do we?

Watched by the other two, ALMA gets up and crosses to the fireplace where she takes a gold cigarette case and lighter from the mantle piece. DOLORES lays her parcels on a convenient table and starts to remove her gloves. CRISPIN hasn't moved.

DOLORES: You turn the whole house into some sort of... *(She waves her hand)* ...vast boudoir.

ALMA: *(Tapping her cigarette against the case)* It IS my house.

DOLORES: Is that meant to be some sort of implied threat?

The cigarette lighter snaps open. ALMA lights her cigarette. DOLORES stares at her sister's back and raises an eyebrow, decides it is better not to say anymore and turns to CRISPIN.

Well at least you're glad to see me.

Nothing from CRISPIN.

Aren't you?

CRISPIN smiles sweetly.

ALMA: Is he wagging his tail? *(Without turning around)* Crispin, do go and put some clothes on, there's a good boy.

DOLORES: Here...

She holds out a brightly patterned menswear shop carrier bag. CRISPIN takes it.

CRISPIN: Thank you.

DOLORES: No reward?

ALMA: Generosity has its own reward.

But CRISPIN kisses DOLORES' cheek. She tries to kiss him on the mouth, but without making it too obvious, he evades her.

What is it?

CRISPIN: I haven't looked yet.

DOLORES: They said at the shop, if you didn't like it, you could take it back and change it. Do you like it?

CRISPIN: I haven't looked yet have I?

ALMA: What are you waiting for? Christmas? You shouldn't spoil him so, Dolores. You're forever buying him things.

DOLORES: He is my nephew.

ALMA: That's no reason to spoil him.

DOLORES: My only nephew.

ALMA: That still doesn't give you the right to spoil him.

DOLORES: He's the only one in this family who ever thinks of me. I bought him a little present. I thought he

	needed cheering up. It's only his mother, I suppose, who must give him things. I haven't anyone else on whom to spend my money.
ALMA:	Do I have to remind you? You also have a niece. Why don't you spoil her a little? Talk of the devil.

CHARLOTTE has entered the room. She is about a year younger than CRISPIN, an attractive girl in her way though not as beautiful as either mother or her brother.

CHARLOTTE:	What a day, what a day. *(Looking around)* Been another family tiff has there? *(She waits, no one moves)* And who is judging who? *(She waits)* No answer was the stern reply. Oh, well... *(She turns to a mirror)* Did you have a good day, Charlotte? *(She touches an eyelid)* You're looking a little tired, dear, a little peaky.
DOLORES:	It's been that kind of a day for most of us. Have you had a rough time?
CHARLOTTE:	A rough old time. Today has been, if anyone is interested, a brute. The brute to end all brutes.
DOLORES:	Mine too. Worse I shouldn't wonder. *(She shuffles over to the sofa)* I must have a sit down before I go upstairs. Some people do have it so lucky.
ALMA:	We've heard that one before.
CHARLOTTE:	And no doubt you'll hear it again.
ALMA:	And again and again.
DOLORES:	*(To CHARLOTTE)* Don't you turn against me.
ALMA:	No one is turning against you. I'd be obliged, Dolores, if you didn't talk such rubbish in front of the children.
CHARLOTTE:	Children!

DOLORES: I know we're all feeling the strain, Alma, but…

ALMA: I am going to see to the dinner. While I am out will someone please change the record? There, there, Dolores, no one means to be unkind to you.

ALMA goes out, closing the door behind her.

CHARLOTTE: What was all that about?

DOLORES: Aren't you ever going to look at your present, Crispin?

CHARLOTTE: Oh, so that's it. Big brother is being spoilt again.

DOLORES: That's not true. I bought him a little present that's all. Is that a crime? What's so unusual in that?

CHARLOTTE: Nothing unusual. That's the trouble.

CRISPIN has opened the carrier bag and takes out a shirt box in which is an expensive lace fronted shirt in a cellophane packet.

DOLORES: Do you like it?

CHRIS: Yes I do. Thank you, aunt.

DOLORES: *(Beaming)* I thought you might wear it tomorrow.

Both children turn to look at her.

Well, why not?

CHARLOTTE: Do you think it's… well, quite the right thing? For this particular occasion?

DOLORES: I don't see why not.

CHARLOTTE: It's a little flamboyant? Not that it isn't a beautiful shirt.

DOLORES:	And he will look beautiful in it. Won't you, my darling? For me?
CHARLOTTE:	The occasion isn't for you.
DOLORES:	Whatever the occasion there is no reason why he shouldn't go looking himself.
CHARLOTTE:	He is certainly not going in the nude.
DOLORES:	That is not...! Let's not have a family debate on the subject. I'm tired. *(She gets up)* If he doesn't want to wear the shirt...
CRISPIN:	I didn't say that.
DOLORES:	Then he needn't wear it.

She heads for the door just as there is a scream from somewhere downstairs. They all turn towards the door. There is another scream, closer this time. DOLORES and CHARLOTTE both turn to look at CRISPIN. There is a third scream right outside the door which is flung open and ALMA hurls herself into the room, slams the door behind her and leans against it, one hand on her breast, gasping for breath. CRISPIN steps towards the door.

ALMA:	I could kill you, Crispin, I really could.
CRISPIN:	Where is it?
ALMA:	I don't know. Following me upstairs more than likely.
CRISPIN:	I doubt that. But, if you'll stand aside, I'll go put it away.
ALMA:	Who let it out?
CRISPIN:	Nobody?
ALMA:	Then what's it doing in the hall?

CRISPIN: I don't know. Must've let itself out.

ALMA: I nearly trod on it. Oh, my heart. If I get another fright like that I'll pass out for good, I promise you.

CRISPIN: Which one is it?

ALMA: How do I know? One of the biggest naturally. It's a monster. It was lying curled up under the telephone table. It was lying in wait for me! I tell you I nearly trod on it. My foot was... *(She holds up her hand, thumb and forefinger together)* that much... that much off it. *(She shudders)* Now you listen to me, Crispin...

CRISPIN: They're great escapologists you know. *(Accusing)* Someone's been down there and tampered with them.

ALMA: No one in their right senses would go anywhere near them.

CHARLOTTE: *(To Crispin)* Which means you are not in your right senses.

ALMA: If he doesn't go and get rid of it this instant, he won't be.

CRISPIN: If you'll move away from the door I'll go.

ALMA: *(Hugging the door)* You won't let it in!

CRISPIN waits.

CRISPIN: Well, what are we going to do? All sit around here and wait for it to disappear?

Reluctantly ALMA moves away from the door.

Thank you.

He goes out, closing the door behind him.

CHARLOTTE: Maybe it's gone out into the garden.

DOLORES and ALMA turn to look at her.

It could climb a creeper and get in through the window.

For a moment the two women continue to stare at CHARLOTTE and then they, managing to control a combined shriek, they head for a French window each, slam, and bolt them. Then they turn back and face the room.

ALMA: Do they climb?

CHARLOTTE: Of course they do. Haven't you heard of them dropping out of branches on top of people?

ALMA: They've got to go. I'll phone the zoo first thing in the morning and have them taken away. They have got to go.

CHARLOTTE: If they go, Crispin goes.

There is a moments silence as this sinks in.

DOLORES: Come and sit down dear. You've had a nasty shock.

She tries to take ALMA's arm but ALMA pulls away.

ALMA: I don't want to sit down. I want a cigarette.

She gets her cigarettes and lighter.

DOLORES: I must admit, quite frankly, I've always thought them rather strange things for a young man to keep. Especially a young man like Crispin.

ALMA: No more strange than his father keeping butterflies. Far healthier I would say.

CHARLOTTE: What's wrong with keeping butterflies?

ALMA: I do not wish to discuss it.

DOLORES: At least butterflies don't sit under telephone tables and leap out at you.

ALMA: It didn't leap out at me. I never said anything about it leaping. I might have leapt. In fact I did. I broke the world high jump record from a standing position.

DOLORES: They really should be kept safely under lock and key. I wonder how it got out. What's the matter, dear?

ALMA: I've just had the most horrifying thought.

DOLORES: What?

ALMA: It might have got to mother. Think of that.

CHARLOTTE: Fat lot she would care.

ALMA: Oh, Charlotte! It might have got your grandmother!

DOLORES: *(Distressed)* Oh, dear.

ALMA: What a newspaper story that would have made.

DOLORES: Do you think he is breaking a bye-law, keeping them in the house? One of those subsection paragraphs that no one ever reads until it's too late?

ALMA: What's happening out there?

DOLORES: Maybe it's wandered off and he can't find it.

CHARLOTTE: I'll go and see.

ALMA: Don't you dare open that door! Don't you dare open it until the all clear.

DOLORES: I'm sure he's breaking a bye-law. I really don't see, I cannot understand, how anyone who loves him so much can allow him such dangerous idiosyncrasies.

ALMA: Better than letting him have a motor bike.

DOLORES: He never wanted a motor bike. He's never mentioned a motor bike.

ALMA: Or a car. Getting himself all mashed up on the roads.

DOLORES: He was always such a normal boy. Didn't he want to be a policeman? And an engine driver? And fireman?

ALMA: Oh, my God!

CHARLOTTE: What now?

ALMA: The roast. The potatoes will be done to a crisp. I don't see that it's so funny. The rare occasions, the very rare occasions when I do love my son, is when he threatens me with... with his... what's that?

DOLORES: It's a shirt.

ALMA: That was the present.

DOLORES: *(Defensively)* Yes.

ALMA: Very nice.

DOLORES: I thought he could wear it tomorrow.

ALMA: You're not serious.

DOLORES: Why ever not?

15

ALMA: Because he is wearing his black suit tomorrow. You know I had one made up for him. A new black suit. He cannot possibly wear that shirt with his black suit.

DOLORES: It will go beautifully with his black suit. I chose it especially.

ALMA: He is not wearing that shirt tomorrow and that's the end of it.

CHARLOTTE: When you two have quite finished fighting over the body of Crispin hadn't we better try and find out what's going on? I want a bath before we eat and I'm sure Aunt Dolores would like one as well. She has been getting a little heated.

DOLORES: I don't find that remark in the best of taste.

ALMA: We will wait here until Crispin comes back and reassures me that all is well.

They wait.

CHARLOTTE: It might have eaten him.

ALMA: If you're going to talk, Charlotte, then talk sense.

They wait.

CHARLOTTE: It might have eaten grandmother.

ALMA: CHARLOTTE!

DOLORES: I don't know how he can ever bear to handle them. Brrrr! A boy without a blemish touching things like that.

CHARLOTTE: They're very beautiful in their own way – some of them.

DOLORES: I've had nightmares over it many a time I can tell

	you. They've always turned against him and he has always come to me.
ALMA:	Why should he come to you?
DOLORES:	This is in my dream. I've heard him crying out for me. Then he's come creeping into my bed to be protected from the monsters. And I protect him. Then, suddenly, one of them is right there.
CHARLOTTE:	Then what happens?
DOLORES:	That's the point when I always wake up, my heart pounding. He'll never get married you know. No wife will ever put up with him, not for a moment.
ALMA:	What's he doing out there?
CHARLOTTE:	Give him a chance, mother. When he's caught it he has to take it back to the basement. And he'll probably have a look around while he's down there.
DOLORES:	Wretched things. They have beastly habits.
CHARLOTTE:	You know nothing about them.
ALMA:	Putting it mildly, they are a nightmare. And think of all the money they cost.
DOLORES:	Do you begrudge it him?
ALMA:	I don't begrudge my children anything.
DOLORES:	Then why are you complaining?
ALMA:	You're not exactly happy about the state of affairs.
DOLORES:	Yes I know. But after all, it is the first time one of them has actually got out.
ALMA:	Whether they actually get out or not is completely

besides the point. They're there. *(Pointing vigorously towards the floor)* Down there.

CHARLOTTE: All right, so they are there. Maybe it would help if we all tried to accept that fact that they're in the house whether we like it or not. No one is going to force or persuade Crispin to get rid of them so let's learn to live with them.

ALMA: And precisely what do you think we have been doing?

DOLORES: Trying to do.

CHARLOTTE: After all, we've had to learn to live with ourselves and Crispin, more or less. Perhaps you ought to make friends with them, love them.

ALMA: Aha! It's "you" all of a sudden. We this and we that but you make friends with them. I haven't noticed any particular anxiety on your part to make friends with them.

She gives a little shriek and backs away from the door. The others turn to see that it has opened a few inches. They all stand staring at it but nothing happens. All three back away a little more.

Crispin? *(Silence)* Crispin, is that you? *(Silence)* Come along now Crispin, don't play the fool. *(Silence)* Crispin!

The door opens wider and a head looks in.

ALMA:
CHARLOTTE: Fanny!
DOLORES:

FANNY: Yes, I am here.

ALMA: What on earth are you playing at?

FANNY: Madam? I can come in please?

ALMA: Yes yes, come in and close the door.

FANNY does so.

ALMA: What were you doing out there?

FANNY: Pardon?

ALMA: Oh, never mind. Did you see Crispin when you came in?

FANNY: No, I never seen him.

DOLORES: Never saw him, dear.

FANNY: Pardon?

ALMA: He wasn't in the hall?

FANNY: No.

ALMA: Dining room?

FANNY: No.

CHARLOTTE: Then he must be in the basement.

FANNY: You want I should find him?

ALMA: No thank you. *(She heads for the door)* You may come and give me a hand in the kitchen. I'm certainly going to need one. Do you mind?

FANNY: No, I don't mind.

ALMA: I mean, it's not contrary to union rules or anything.

FANNY: Pardon?

ALMA: Good. I dread to think what state that oven is in.

She goes out, followed by a bewildered FANNY. DOLORES retires once more to the sofa.

DOLORES: I don't like that girl.

CHARLOTTE: Why not?

DOLORES: She's much too forward. The way she chases after Crispin... upstairs and downstairs... It's positively... obscene.

CHARLOTTE: Aren't you exaggerating just a little?

DOLORES: Am I? Am I? Hmn!

She crosses her arms over her chest and rubs a shoulder, her attitude meant to imply, 'Just you wait and see.'

CHARLOTTE: I wouldn't blame her if she were.

DOLORES: Charlotte! Crispin is your brother.

CHARLOTTE: So?

DOLORES: It's not her position.

CHARLOTTE: What does that mean?

DOLORES: Would you like to see your one and only brother snared by a foreign maid?

CHARLOTTE: She is not a maid, aunt. She is an au pair.

DOLORES: She's... German! And you know what they are like.

CHARLOTTE: No I don't know what they are like and I still think you are exaggerating.

DOLORES: Did you notice how eager she was to find him a moment ago?

CHARLOTTE: Perhaps it's to her bed he would like to go in his troubles.

DOLORES: Charlotte!

CHARLOTTE: Why not? She's a very attractive girl.

DOLORES: Crispin could never, never love a girl like that.

CHARLOTTE: Who's talking about love? Anyway, don't you think Crispin should decide for himself who he can and can't love?

DOLORES: Well of course he is his own master.

CHARLOTTE: Yes.

FANNY enters the room to a frosty silence.

FANNY: Madam forgot her cigarettes.

FANNY looks from CHARLOTTE to DOLORES' stiff, unyielding back and then looks for the cigarettes, finds them and starts for the door.

DOLORES: No evening class this evening, Fanny?

FANNY: No. That is why I am here.

She waits, but as there is nothing more forthcoming, starts to go.

I take the cigarettes to madam.

DOLORES: We shouldn't be having a roast tonight.

CHARLOTTE: Oh?

DOLORES: Well, it doesn't seem decent somehow.

CHARLOTTE: What should we be having?

DOLORES: Well, something plain.

CHARLOTTE: You couldn't get any plainer than one of mother's roasts.

DOLORES: Don't be flippant, Charlotte. Not tonight.

CHARLOTTE: I thought you were going upstairs.

DOLORES: I must have a sit down for a minute. All that excitement. You forget, Charlotte, I am one of the older generation, I can't be on the go all the time. It's bad enough that I have to go out to work everyday. I'll just sit here for a minute and calm down. Weren't you going to take a bath?

CHARLOTTE: Yes. *(She dithers for a moment)* I'll run yours as soon as I'm finished, shall I?

DOLORES: Thank you, dear, that is kind. One does so appreciate little acts of kindness. These days there are far too few and we should all be kind to each other at a time like this. That is why one appreciates someone like Crispin so much, for the comfort he brings. There is not so much as an ounce of harm in his whole bo… being. The world is a much better place for people like that.

She dabs at an eye with a diminutive hankie.

CHARLOTTE: Are you crying?

DOLORES: *(Straightening up)* No. No, after all these years it is too late for tears.

CHARLOTTE: You sound like a pop song. All right, you sit there and be a happy little martyr.

DOLORES: It's all right for you. You're still young, in the first bloom, you don't know yet what lies ahead of you. And your mother, she's alright. She got married. She has her children to be a comfort in her old age.

CHARLOTTE: There's very little guarantee of that.

DOLORES: She has her memories.

CHARLOTTE: And so have you. Albums full of them.

DOLORES: *(Going her own sweet way)* A time like this is a time for memories.

CHARLOTTE: You've scrubbed Crispin's back in the bath as many, if not more times, than mother ever has.

DOLORES: What have I got? Who will I have? I know I will end up all alone, probably in some awful home where everyone will be unkind to me. Where I'll be as wretched as I can possibly be.

CHARLOTTE: If that is what you want you're heading fast in the right direction.

DOLORES: Thank you, dear. I knew I could rely on you to cheer me up.

This time she really does start to cry.

CHARLOTTE: That's right, let it all out. You'll feel much better for it. After all, you have been very, very brave.

DOLORES: Why doesn't Crispin come back? He would be a comfort. He would understand.

CHARLOTTE: Would he?

DOLORES: Oh, You're very smart, young lady. Very smart. Very bright and with it. You can cast aspersions on other people.

CHARLOTTE: I haven't said a thing.

DOLORES: It's your whole attitude.

CHARLOTTE: Tell me about my attitude.

DOLORES: Oh, why don't you go and have your bath?

CHARLOTTE: *(Peering closely)* You'd better do a quick repair job. You wouldn't like Crispin so young and fair to come in and see you looking like that. Now would you?

DOLORES sits glaring at her niece. Her fingers itch to slap the serene young face so close to hers.

DOLORES: God will punish you.

CHARLOTTE: He has given you personal assurance has he?

DOLORES: Don't be irreverent. It's not smart and it's not funny.

CRISPIN enters. He has changed into a light sports shirt and slacks but is still padding about barefoot.

CRISPIN: What's not funny?

CHARLOTTE:
DOLORES: Is everythi...?

They look at each other.

CHARLOTTE: Everything all right?

CRISPIN nods happily and crosses over to pick up and fiddle with his new shirt.

DOLORES: *(Hissing)* I thought you were going to have...

CHARLOTTE: All right. What's the big rush?

DOLORES: Oh, no hurry at all. It's just that, if you don't go now, there won't be time for both of us before supper.

But, instead of going, CHARLOTTE crosses to CRISPIN. He looks up and smiles at her. He puts down the shirt and they stand facing each other, each with their arms about each others waist.

CHARLOTTE: Are you going out this evening?

DOLORES: I should hope not. Not this evening.

CHARLOTTE brushes back a wisp of hair off Crispin's face.

CHARLOTTE: Are you?

CRISPIN shakes his head.

Are you upset?

CRISPIN: No, not particularly. Should I be? Hmn... yes, I suppose I should really. Except that it doesn't seem real somehow. It hasn't gone home yet. Maybe after tomorrow.

DOLORES is growing more and more agitated watching and being completely left out of this very private little scene between brother and sister.

DOLORES: *(Warning)* Charlotte.

CRISPIN: Did you want to go out?

CHARLOTTE: No.

DOLORES: Neither of you should even be thinking of such a thing. Your mother needs you. Don't you understand that? It wouldn't be right for you to go out this evening. It would be most disrespectful.

CRISPIN: We're not going out.

He kisses CHARLOTTE on the nose and they rub noses.

DOLORES: I knew you at least would know where your duty

lies.

CRISPIN: I don't particularly feel like going out.

CHARLOTTE laughs and kisses CRISPIN on the neck. He rolls his head, enjoying her nuzzling into him. CHARLOTTE smiling happily, turns to leave the room, pauses to look at DOLORES, and goes out. DOLORES is left facing CRISPIN and not looking too happy about it. She searches for a starting point.

DOLORES: Well... and what have you done today?

CRISPIN: Nothing.

DOLORES: Come and sit by me and tell me all about it.

CRISPIN: About nothing?

DOLORES has sat on the sofa, her hand on the seat beside her and CRISPIN moves forward. She is almost panting in expectation but he stops by the small table, selects a piece of crème de menthe.

DOLORES: You must have done something today.

CRISPIN: I haven't done anything. I lay around all day.

DOLORES: You stayed in to look after your mother. Kept her company.

CRISPIN shrugs. If that's the way she wants it.

I think that it is most commendable.

CRISPIN: I'll award myself something.

He takes another crème de menthe. DOLORES moves up close and takes the sweetmeat dish from him, putting it back on the table.

DOLORES: You'll spoil your appetite. That is, if there is anything to eat.

CRISPIN: Might there not be? I do hope not. I'm hungry.

DOLORES: For what?

CRISPIN: Food of course. What do you suppose? Good, solid, nourishing, delicious, vitamin packed food.

DOLORES: Nothing else?

CRISPIN: Not that I know of.

DOLORES: Don't you feel, Crispin, that there is something terribly lacking in your life?

CRISPIN: No. I'm very happy.

DOLORES: Are you? Are you really?

CRISPIN: Are you trying to raise doubts about it?

DOLORES: I had a word with one of the directors today... at work... I asked him about you.

CRISPIN: Asked him what about me?

DOLORES: Crispin, you knew I was going to. We discussed it the other evening. You and I and you mother.

CRISPIN: We didn't discuss it. You talked about it. Mother and I listened.

DOLORES: Or pretended to listen.

CRISPIN: No, we listened.

DOLORES: I really don't know why I even bother.

CRISPIN: *(Smiling sweetly)* Because you worry about me.

DOLORES: Crispin, you know we have a training scheme, the company I mean. I am sure they would accept you.

>
> Oh, Crispin... *(She has moved up behind him and now her hands are on his shoulders)*... Crispin,... it would be marvellous to... it would... to have you at work... to be with me there, every day.

He drums his fingers on her hands for a moment.

CRISPIN: Yes.

And moves away, changing direction after a few steps for the bonbon dish.

DOLORES: *(A little too sharply)* And to get you out of this house.

CRISPIN: *(Turning)* Don't you like this house, aunt?

DOLORES: That's not what I said.

CRISPIN: *(Rummaging in the dish)* I love it.

DOLORES: What about the people in it?

CRISPIN: Oh, yes. I love them too.

DOLORES: *(Moving in)* Crispin, accept the interview. After all, you can't live off your mother for the rest of your life.

CRISPIN: Why not?

DOLORES: Why not? Because it... it... it isn't right.

CRISPIN: If mother is quite happy with the arrangement you shouldn't question it. Are you trying to make me angry?

DOLORES: No! Of course not.

CRISPIN: You're trying to upset me.

DOLORES: No, believe me, my darling, I am not. Never.

CRISPIN:	I am perfectly provided for while mother is here. And, after she is gone, I continue to live off her royalties for another fifty years. After all, people are not going to stop having babies. Babies are not going to stop growing into children and children are not going to stop learning to read. At least, I hope not. So where is the problem? After all, I was the inspiration for mother's best selling character; I deserve something for that, don't I?
DOLORES:	I won't say another word.

CRISPIN smiles and turns his back to the bonbon dish. DOLORES moves in a step or two.

	Crispin... what would you say to... that is, after tomorrow... *(Moves closer)*... why don't we take a holiday?
CRISPIN:	Go away?
DOLORES:	Yes.
CRISPIN:	Just the two of us?
DOLORES:	*(Closer)* Yes.
CRISPIN:	*(Moving away)* Where would we go?
DOLORES:	Anywhere you like. I'll pay for it. *(Moving in)* Majorca? Corfu? Venice?
CRISPIN:	*(Moving away)* Some romantic place.
DOLORES:	Yes. Yes. You say. Anywhere.

She is breathing hard again as she waits for an answer.

	Well? Wouldn't you like that?
CRISPIN:	I don't know.

DOLORES: Say you'll think about it.

CRISPIN: I'll think about it.

DOLORES: Oh, my darling...

She is too close now and her self restraint is falling to pieces but, at the moment, ALMA enters.

ALMA: You will be relieved to hear that dinner; well part of it anyway, is saved.

CRISPIN: I never knew it was in danger.

ALMA: It was through you we nearly lost it.

CRISPIN: Why? What have I done?

ALMA: What have you been doing? The two of you look like a pair of conspirators.

CRISPIN: Aunt Dolores has just asked me to go away on holiday with her.

ALMA: Oh, has she?

DOLORES: It was only a suggestion, Alma... an idea.

ALMA: I am sure if Crispin feels he wants a holiday he only has to say so and he can come away with me.

CRISPIN: I don't particularly want a holiday.

ALMA: That settles it then. Fanny should have finished in the kitchen by now, shall we eat? Where's Charlotte?

DOLORES: She went to take a bath.

CRISPIN: A what!

But, before DOLORES can repeat it, there is a scream, this time from upstairs. They all turn to the door. There is another scream, nearer, and then a third as CHARLOTTE belts into the room. She is wrapped in a bath towel. There is a moment and then.

CHARLOTTE: There is a bloody great crocodile in the bath!

ALMA and DOLORES turn on CRISPIN.

ALMA:
DOLORES: CRISPIN!

Blackout.

Act Two

ALMA, DOLORES, CHARLOTTE and CRISPIN exactly as we left them.

CRISPIN: It's not a crocodile. It's an alligator. And it's only a baby.

CHARLOTTE: Some baby.

ALMA: Crispin, don't you think this is going a bit too far?

CRISPIN: What is?

ALMA: Well, I mean! Keep your pets in the basement by all means but in the bath!

CRISPIN: I had nowhere else to put her.

DOLORES: Keeping them in the basement is bad enough.

CRISPIN: They don't bother you, not in the basement.

DOLORES: They're there and we know they are there. Deliveries of live rats to the front door. Live mice. *(She shudders violently)* God knows what the neighbours must think.

CRISPIN: They are delivered in plain packages. The neighbours don't even know.

But, having been betrayed by her favourite, DOLORES insists on pushing it.

DOLORES: Packages with holes.

CRISPIN: Of course. They've got to breathe haven't they?

DOLORES: And what if the rats were to escape? Rats, all over the house.

At the thought of it her knees suddenly buckle and she sits down heavily.

I feel quite faint. Packages with holes are not plain packages. Why can't they eat dead things like everyone else? And do you know what they do with the bits they can't digest? They cough them up in little bundles.

ALMA: For God's sake, Dolores! This is not a natural history lesson.

DOLORES: Don't shout at me, Alma. I am your sister.

ALMA: Crispin, snakes are your particularity…

DOLORES: Peculiarity.

ALMA: Why have you suddenly gone and bought a crocodile?

CRISPIN: Alligator.

ALMA: Alligator.

CRISPIN: I happened to be in Harrods and I took a fancy to her. Harrods delivered her this morning.

CHARLOTTE: That's all very well, brother of mine, but just how are we supposed to take a bath?

CRISPIN: She's very friendly. She won't hurt you.

CHARLOTTE: You mean you expect me to take a bath with it?

ALMA: No, Crispin, it simply won't do.

CHARLOTTE: I should say!

ALMA: You'll just have to take it back to Harrods first thing in the morning and explain to them that you made a mistake. They're very understanding.

CRISPIN: I can't take it tomorrow.

ALMA: Oh, no, I forgot. Well the day after that then. In the meantime you had better find somewhere else to keep it because it can't stay in the bath.

CHARLOTTE: I know, what about the inflatable swimming pool?

CRISPIN: It's punctured. We put an arrow through it didn't we? Last summer.

ALMA: Then mend the puncture.

CRISPIN: With what?

ALMA: Don't be deliberately exasperating, Crispin. There is a cycle repair outfit somewhere in the house.

CRISPIN: That won't be any use. It hasn't been used for at least – I don't know – nine? Ten years? And anyway I don't know where it is.

ALMA: Crispin, apart from snakes in the basement and, at the moment a crocodile in the bath, this is, in all other respects, a perfectly normal English household – I think. There is a cupboard under the stairs. There is a cupboard in the nursery. There is an attic. In these you will find the usual accretions of years of family history. There are beach balls, there are footballs, and there are cricket bats, tennis rackets, fishing rods and a lot of perished rubber that was once something. There are old discarded hats, Wellingtons and dolls without heads, paint boxes, pencil boxes and lamp shades with cigarette burns in them. There is a studded trunk and a number of suitcases, drawing books and school books, a birdcage, roller skates, ice skates and a table tennis net, ludo, monopoly, odd bits of lead piping and, no doubt, a holed ball cock. Now will you please do some research among that lot and come up with (a) an inflatable swimming pool, (b) a cycle repair outfit and (c) bring them together to make a new home for your crocodile.

FANNY appears at the door.

FANNY:	The dinner is set, madam.
ALMA:	Thank you, Fanny. *(To Crispin)* Do it first thing after dinner. Charlotte, for goodness sake go and put on some clothes. You can't sit down at table like that.

CHARLOTTE disappears.

                    Dolores? Are you coming or aren't you?

DOLORES gets up and ALMA heads for the door.

                    Come along, Crispin, it's on the table and it will get cold.

CRISPIN:	I'm not coming.
ALMA:	I beg your pardon?
CRISPIN:	*(Sitting)* I'm not coming.
ALMA:	And why not?
CRISPIN:	I want to think.
ALMA:	What you mean is you want to sulk.
DOLORES:	You told me a moment ago that you were hungry.
CRISPIN:	Put it on one side. I'll have it when I'm ready.

ALMA: Come and have it at once and don't be silly. *(No response)* All right, suit yourself. Come along, Dolores. *(As she passes her)* Fanny.

ALMA sweeps out followed by FANNY who doesn't go until she has cast a long lingering look at CRISPIN. DOLORES dithers until sure the others have gone.

DOLORES: Crispin, you aren't angry with me are you, darling?

CRISPIN: Don't call me that.

DOLORES: Oh, dear. You are angry. Please don't be. I'm sorry, I didn't mean to…

CRISPIN: Your food will be getting cold. You'll get skin on your gravy and horrid congealed fat on your plate. Your peas will wrinkle like fingertips in the bath tub and your potatoes go all hard.

DOLORES: I don't care. How can I possibly go downstairs knowing how upset you are? I couldn't eat a thing. Shall I keep you company until you feel better? *(No response)* Don't be cruel, Crispin, it's not in your nature to be cruel. *(No response)* I thought you would appreciate a lovely holiday by the sea. *(No response)* Just tell me I'm forgiven and I'll go.

CRISPIN: You're forgiven.

DOLORES: That doesn't sound as though you mean it.

CRISPIN moves quickly up to her, pecks her on the cheek and, just as quickly, moves away again.

CRISPIN: There… you're forgiven. *(He is moving towards the windows)* Who closed the windows?

DOLORES: Er… we did.

CRISPIN: *(Opening one)* Why? *(No answer)* On a hot

	summer evening. *(He turns to her and laughs)* Did you and mother expect things to come creepy crawling through the windows?
DOLORES:	Are you coming down now?
CRISPIN:	Not yet.
DOLORES:	You can't stay up here all on your own.
CRISPIN:	Why on earth not? If I get lonely I'll go and sit with granny. She wouldn't kick up a stink about my pets. She'd understand.
DOLORES:	Yes, I know I know. We were a bit hasty. It's… it's the strain. Crispin, you have to understand that. It will all be different once tomorrow is over. We'll be a happy family again, you'll see.

There is a shout from down stairs.

ALMA:	Dolores? Are you coming or aren't you? Your food is getting stone cold.
DOLORES:	Coming, dear.
ALMA:	What on earth has got into this family tonight?

A door slams. DOLORES dithers a moment and then decides she had better go down before there really is a riot.

DOLORES:	I'm going down then.
CRISPIN:	Bon appétit.
DOLORES:	Ooooooh…

With a faint moan she disappears. CRISPIN stands for a moment. He is hungry but his pride is not going to allow him to leave the room. He throws himself on to the sofa and curls up into a little ball. There is a moment of absolute stillness, and then a figure appears at the window, stands there for a second, then a hand pushes the net curtain aside and ANGELA looks into the room. As it is apparently deserted she steps in.

ANGELA is about eighteen. What she would look like under normal circumstances is anybody's guess, very probably very pretty, but having just climbed a garden wall and a vine, and that after running some distance, she is flushed, grimy, and breathless.

Also she looks like a rag bag to end all ragbags. ANGELA is a late developed flower child though hardly one of nature's innocents. She advances further into the room, still looking around. CRISPIN senses he is not alone and looks up at the moment when ANGELA has her back to him. Seeing the apparition he disappears into the sofa again, curling up into an even tighter ball until, in looking around the room, ANGELA gets too close for comfort and he suddenly sits up.

CRISPIN: What...?

With a shriek, ANGELA leaps in twenty directions at once and clutches her breast. She comes to earth again facing CRISPIN and gasping for breath.

ANGELA:
CRISPIN: What...?

CRISPIN stares at her as she at him.

ANGELA: Oh, what a fright you gave me. *(Pause)* I didn't know there was anyone here. *(She realises this is no justification for her own presence)* I came in through the window. *(This is hardly any justification either)* yes... well... surprised you didn't I? *(Silence)* Of course I didn't mean to. *(Silence. She tries to giggle and a hunching of the shoulders. It doesn't work)* Cat got your tongue? *(Silence)* Why don't you say something? Anything. *(Silence)* I'm Angela.

CRISPIN: What are you doing here?

ANGELA:	Sanctuary! Sanctuary! *(Silence)* I am seeking a temporary refuge.
CRISPIN:	I beg your pardon?
ANGELA:	Hiding. From the fuzz.
CRISPIN:	Are they after you? Why?
ANGELA:	Well, not me in particular. But they're not very particular are they?
CRISPIN:	*(Eyeing her up and down)* No.
ANGELA:	Bloody fascists. As long as they make their requisite number of arrests, to fill their quota I mean.
CRISPIN:	What would happen if you were arrested?
ANGELA:	*(Panic)* That means you're going to hand me over.
CRISPIN:	No it doesn't.
ANGELA:	They'd beat me up more than likely, put the boot in.
CRISPIN:	Do they do that? In England?
ANGELA:	Where've you been all your life? Of course they do. They put the boot in as soon as look at you. They're the same all over the world. All police are fascists. They wouldn't be police otherwise would they?
CRISPIN:	I don't know. Have you been arrested before?
ANGELA:	What?
CRISPIN:	How many times have you been arrested?
ANGELA:	Well... I haven't actually... yet. But friends of mine have.

CRISPIN: *(Nods)* Why are you hiding from them now?

ANGELA: Oh, we've been having a sit in. It got a bit wild. You'll probably see it on the news if you've got a telly.

She looks around for the telly.

CRISPIN: Are you at the college?

ANGELA: That's right.

CRISPIN: And the sit-ins become a run-out.

ANGELA: Certainly not. We have made a strategic withdrawal that's all. Temporary.

CRISPIN: Of course. I'm rather surprised though that the police were called in. I thought college authorities liked to keep this sort of thing in the family, handle it themselves.

ANGELA: They're incapable of handling it. All administrators are bungling incompetents. It was inevitable the fuzz should be called in sooner or later.

CRISPIN: I suppose it was.

ANGELA: One thing you learn about though – bureaucracy moves very slow its purpose to fulfill. You can always keep one step ahead. That's why, of course, it will eventually kill itself. The fuzz will hang about for a while pretending to be efficient then they'll move out and we'll move back in. They can't mismanage the traffic and us at the same time.

CRISPIN: What was the sit-in all about?

ANGELA: Conditions in the college, what else?

CRISPIN: What about them?

ANGELA: They're primitive, man. Positively barbarous. You haven't got any food have you? I'm hungry.

Almost absentmindedly, CRISPIN passes her the bonbon dish. She looks at it and walks away. He puts it down.

CRISPIN: How?

ANGELA: What?

CRISPIN: Primitive.

ANGELA: Well, for a start, there are no decent washing facilities.

CRISPIN laughs, ANGELA reacts, then decides to ignore it.

And as for discipline, they treat us like children. Well we're not children. We want more say in our own affairs. I mean, how the college is run. It is run for our benefit after all.

CRISPIN: So why did you choose this particular house in which to hide.

ANGELA: Handy. I hopped over the wall, up the creeper and in the window. I couldn't find anywhere to get in downstairs. And you can see the garden from the street can't you? Through the gate. So I'll just cool it here till the hue and cry dies down then I'll go. Are you sure you don't have anything to eat? I really am starving. That's another complaint, the canteen. What about downstairs?

CRISPIN: Too many people down there and I don't want to see them at the moment.

ANGELA: Family? You poor kid. I understand, man. Families can be rough, a real drag. Take mine for instance, I couldn't wait to get rid of them.

CRISPIN: I don't think mine would take too kindly to you anyway. Don't sit there!

ANGELA who is about to flop into a chair, looks at him in some surprise.

ANGELA: Why not?

CRISPIN: You're filthy.

ANGELA: I am not.

CRISPIN: You are filthy. I can smell you from here. I can smell bodies. If you must sit then sit on the floor, preferably the wood bit where it's easier to wash.

ANGELA glares at him for a moment and then looks around the room again.

ANGELA: Hmph! I might have expected it.

CRISPIN: Expected what?

ANGELA: That you'd be so – bourgeois.

CRISPIN: That's an old fashion word. Does it still mean anything?

ANGELA: It may not mean anything to the likes of you but to me it still means something.

CRISPIN: Don't talk at me please. I'm not a telephone.

ANGELA: And to thousands – no – millions like me.

CRISPIN: Are there millions like you? No wonder the world smells so bad.

ANGELA: You want to get out into it a bit more often and smell what it's really like. It smells so bad because people like me lift the covers and let the sewer stink out.

Defiantly she plonks herself down in the chair and glares at CRISPIN, defying him to move her. He steps forward, thinks better of it, and stops.

CRISPIN: I think you ought to go. If anyone comes in and finds you here you're for it I can tell you.

ANGELA: Yes? *(She surveys him from the chair)* I'll take my chance if you'll take yours.

He shrugs and moves away.

What's your name?

CRISPIN: *(Turning back)* Why?... Crispin.

ANGELA: Well... Crispin... why don't you relax?

CRISPIN: I'm perfectly at home, thank you.

ANGELA: I know that, but why don't you relax?

CRISPIN: Why don't you go away? I should think the police must have gone back to the traffic by now.

ANGELA: What do you do, Crispin?

CRISPIN: Do?

ANGELA: Yes, do. Everybody does something, more than stand around and breathe.

CRISPIN walks around to where he can look at her from another angle.

CRISPIN: Why do you dress like that?

ANGELA: How am I dressed?

CRISPIN: Like a walking jumble sale.

ANGELA: You really aren't together at all are you?

CRISPIN: Are you?

ANGELA: Tell me, how am I supposed to dress?

CRISPIN: I should think, under that lot, and if you had a really good wash, you might be quite pretty really.

ANGELA: Oh, thanks a lot. A great one with the compliments aren't you? I have no particular wish, thank you very much, to be considered pretty.

CRISPIN: Why not? Pretty people have a distinct advantage in life.

ANGELA: You should know.

CRISPIN: Yes, I do.

ANGELA: Oh, my God. Anyway, prettiness is a facile quality. Beautiful people are the ones that matter. There is a difference you know. And it hasn't got anything to do with having a retrousse nose, or a rosebud mouth. You really do want to get out into the big wide world, Crispin, and find out what it's all about.

CRISPIN: You know of course.

ANGELA: Do you spend all of your time cooped up in this musty, stuffy old tomb?

CRISPIN: Why do you call it that?

ANGELA: Because that's what it is. My God, you can feel the hand of the dead on you wherever you turn. It's creepy, man.

CRISPIN: It's nothing of the kind.

ANGELA: Come to think of it, you're pretty dead yourself, from the navel both ways I shouldn't wonder. Not that you're unattractive, far from it. In fact I think I could rather go for you in a big way. Do you suppose it was fate that brought me through your window?

CRISPIN: Whatever it was I shan't be in the least sorry to have it take you right out again.

ANGELA: *(Looking round)* Yes... with a few minor adjustments like throwing everything out, this wouldn't make too bad a pad. Not bad at all.

CRISPIN: Hey! Someone's coming!

ANGELA leaps out of the chair and scuttles around to crouch behind it just as there is a tap at the door and FANNY looks in.

FANNY: Crispin?

CRISPIN: Yes?

FANNY: Your mother says I am to bring you this.

She enters the room carrying the deflated swimming pool and a puncture repair outfit.

CRISPIN: Oh, thank you.

FANNY: What have you got to do with it?

CRISPIN: According to mother, find a puncture and repair it. *(He starts to examine the pool)* Let's see...

And becomes aware that FANNY is very close, pretending to be interested in the examination but really being much more interested in him. He looks up to see her face three inches from his own.

Have you eaten?

FANNY: No. Not yet. Your mother was finding you these things.

CRISPIN: Hadn't you better go down then?

FANNY: I would like it better to stay and help you with the er....

CRISPIN: Puncture.

FANNY: Puncture.

CRISPIN: You might like it much better. Even I might like it much better. But I doubt whether mother and Charlotte, to say nothing of Aunt Dolores, would like it much better. And so sweet Teuton, to avoid any unnecessary unpleasantness, you had better go and join the Anglo Saxons at the table before world war three breaks out.

FANNY: But I would rather be here with you.

CRISPIN: No.

FANNY: To keep you company?

CRISPIN: No.

FANNY: I must go?

CRISPIN: Yes, Fräulein, I am afraid you must.

CHARLOTTE appears at the door. She has changed for dinner and is on her way down.

CHARLOTTE: Hello hello hello? What have we here? A tete-a-tete? I don't want to break up the party but aren't we all supposed to be downstairs enjoying the burnt offering? Oh, you found it did you?

CRISPIN: Mother found it.

CHARLOTTE: Don't you believe it? Mother knew where it was all along. There is nothing in this house mother doesn't know. It used to be granny who knew absolutely everything. Now it's mother. Will you be able to fix it?

CRISPIN: I haven't found the hole yet.

CHARLOTTE: And you're unlikely to... *(Looking at FANNY)* if your concentration wavers. Crispin?

CRISPIN: Ah, here it is.

CHARLOTTE: Crispin.

CRISPIN: Now to see if there's a big enough patch.

CHARLOTTE: Crispin!

CRISPIN: What?

CHARLOTTE: I've brought home some new designs. I'd like you to take a look at them.

CRISPIN: All right.

CHARLOTTE: They are in my room. Will you come up after dinner?

CRISPIN: Hmn...

CHARLOTTE: Well at least try and sound enthusiastic even if you don't feel it.

CRISPIN: Of course I'd like to see them.

CHARLOTTE: Thank you. You know I feel better, more confident, if I get your approval before I submit them.

FANNY: Could I see them too?

CHARLOTTE: Of course you may – after Crispin. I would prefer him to make his comments without distraction and before he can be influenced in any way.

FANNY opens her mouth to object.

Your being there is quite enough to influence him so contain yourself in patience, Fanny dear.

CRISPIN: What are they?

CHARLOTTE: Beachwear.

CRISPIN: Maybe I'd better bring the pool up with me then.

CHARLOTTE: As long as the crocodile isn't in it.

FANNY: Crocodile?

CHARLOTTE: Oh, you aren't up on the latest addition to the family.

FANNY: Please? I don't understand.

CHARLOTTE: Step into the bathtub dear. You will.

CRISPIN: Have you designed something special in beachwear for Aunt Dolores' holiday?

CHARLOTTE: No. Tell you what, you and I will design her a whole outfit when you come up.

CRISPIN: All right.

CHARLOTTE: Remember Crispin, when we were kids, how we used to spend whole days up in the nursery, drawing? It's as well we had the instinct to burn most of them.

CRISPIN: They weren't very artistic.

CHARLOTTE: Maybe not. More revealing wouldn't you say?

FANNY: Them I would have liked to have seen too.

CHARLOTTE: I'm sure you would.

ALMA bursts into the room.

ALMA: What is going on here? I send someone up on the simplest of errands and I walk in half an hour later on an emergency session of the United Nations.

CRISPIN: Half an hour? You've been experimenting with your time machine again.

ALMA: The food has been on and off the table faster than knickers with perished elastic.

CHARLOTTE:
CRISPIN: *(Both slightly shocked)* Mother!

ALMA: Well, you are both so irritating. Is there no one in this family I can trust? Why I bother to cook for you lot at all I really do not know.

CHARLOTTE: Coming, Crispin?

CRISPIN: Yes. *(Then, remembering ANGELA, he throws a quick glance towards the chair)* Er... No, not yet. I'll fix this first, then the family can use the bath again. Cleanliness, after all, is next to Godliness.

ALMA: When you have quite finished with the proverbs, I am waiting.

CHARLOTTE: Wait no longer, mother dear, we are right behind you.

ALMA: I tell you, compared to me, Patience on her monument is about as serene as a Dervish with St Vitus's dance.

She goes out followed by CHARLOTTE. FANNY stops at the door and comes back.

FANNY: Crispin.

CRISPIN looks up from the pool in which he is pretending to be engrossed.

I had a letter today from my family.

CRISPIN: That's nice. All well I hope.

FANNY: They say they are most happy to see you in Germany.

CRISPIN: Are they?

FANNY: Yes, I am to take you back with me when I go.

CRISPIN: What?

FANNY: I did ask them, my family. I told them they would like you very much and they are happy for you to come stay with us for as long as you like.

CRISPIN is taken aback by this which is all news to him and doesn't know quite what to say next.

CRISPIN: Well, that's very nice of your family. If I er... if I ever think of coming to Germany, I'll take them up on it.

FANNY: Oh, but you must come.

CRISPIN: Must I? Why?

FANNY: *(Moving in)* Crispin...

ALMA: *(Off)* Fanny?

FANNY: *(Stamping her foot)* Pferdapfel!

CRISPIN: You'd better go down before there is trouble.

FANNY: (Almost wringing her hands in frustration) Crispin... (But decides discretion is the better part of valour and goes, not without a long, lingering look from the door which evokes another)

ALMA: Fanny!

FANNY *disappears very fast leaving CRISPIN staring at the empty doorway. ANGELA comes creaking out of her hiding place, stretching her cramped limbs and limping a little.*

ANGELA: Man...

CRISPIN *jumps.*

Have you got troubles!

CRISPIN: Oh, yes. I'd forgotten you.

ANGELA: I'm not talking about me, man. I'm talking about you. You!

CRISPIN *starts work on mending the puncture.*

Split, man.

CRISPIN: What?

ANGELA: Split.

CRISPIN: No, it's punctured. We shot an arrow into it last summer.

ANGELA *runs her hand through her hair.*

ANGELA: Are there any more in the house?

CRISPIN: Any more what?

ANGELA: People. If that's what you want to call them.

CRISPIN: Oh, yes. There's my Aunt Dolores. She's downstairs.

	You didn't see her. And there's granny.
ANGELA:	Any more?
CRISPIN:	No, that's the lot as far as people go. Then there are the snakes.
ANGELA:	Snakes?
CRISPIN:	Yes, snakes. I keep them in the basement. They're in vivariums so they're quite happy. I go down last thing at night and talk to them, make a fuss of them, turn out the lights. The heating stays on all night of course. They're very susceptible to pneumonia. Would you like to see them?
ANGELA:	Not particularly. How many are there?
CRISPIN:	Only four. They are called Alma, Charlotte, Dolores and Fanny. Mother and the others don't know that of course. I don't think they would see it quite my way. I shall call the... what did you ay your name was?
ANGELA:	Angela.
CRISPIN:	I shall call the alligator, Angela.
ANGELA:	I'm highly honoured.
CRISPIN:	Do you want to see them?
ANGELA:	No thank you. I'm not exactly in a snake mood right now.
CRISPIN:	Oh, do. They're very beautiful you know. They're fascinating. I can watch them for hours even when they're not doing anything. At least, it looks as though they're not doing anything. In fact, they're probably doing quite a lot really if you knew what it was. Ruminating in a sort of reptilian kind of way. How do you suppose animals think? In

	pictures?
ANGELA:	You're possessed. Do you know that? I think you ought to think more about yourself and less about your snakes.
CRISPIN:	Who says I don't think about myself?
ANGELA:	Only in connection with your family. You should think even less of your family. Split, man. You got to get out of this place. This place is unhealthy. This place is stultifying.
CRISPIN:	You don't know what you are talking about.
ANGELA:	I do, I do! Believe me, I do.
CRISPIN:	Come down and see my snakes.
ANGELA:	I don't want to see your snakes.
CRISPIN:	I have two boa constrictors and a regal python and a horned viper.
ANGELA:	Thank you, a very nice selection but I still don't want to see them.
CRISPIN:	You don't have to touch them. Are you afraid?
ANGELA:	No. Lacking in interest.
CRISPIN:	I see. Isn't it time you were going?
ANGELA:	*(Kneeling beside him)* Listen... Crispin...
CRISPIN:	Actually, the horned viper is male but I thought, what the hell, the others are all women and, When Fanny came to stay with us, I automatically called it Fanny.
ANGELA:	Crispin...

She puts out a tentative hand but he withdraws.

CRISPIN: Boas and pythons aren't poisonous of course. They crush, and suffocate. That breaks the bones of course. Then they swallow their victims' whole.

ANGELA: Victims?

CRISPIN: What?

ANGELA: Victims. You said victims.

CRISPIN: Did I? *(He shrugs and goes back to his work)* What would you call something that's…?

ANGELA: That's what, Crispin?

CRISPIN: Eaten of course. Something alive that's eaten.

For a moment she watches him work.

ANGELA: Do you ever go out?

CRISPIN: What a stupid question. Of course I do.

ANGELA: But you always come back to this place.

CRISPIN: Why do you say it like that? Why do you call it 'this place?' Why don't you say 'here?' What other place should I go to?

ANGELA: Well, if you wanted to, you could come to our place.

CRISPIN: What?

ANGELA: Why not? We've got this swinging pad in the Goldhawk road.

CRISPIN: Who is we?

ANGELA: Well, it's like a little community.

CRISPIN:	Mixed?
ANGELA:	Of course.
CRISPIN:	A sort of monkery.

He is quite please with his little joke and chortles to himself.

ANGELA:	Everything is shared of course.
CRISPIN:	Everything?
ANGELA:	*(Firmly, staring him straight in the eye)* Everything.
CRISPIN:	How many of you are there?
ANGELA:	Who bothers to count?
CRISPIN:	You mean people just come and go as they please?
ANGELA:	That's right, man. Everyone is free.
CRISPIN:	It must be very disorganised.
ANGELA:	That's the whole beauty of it. Man, this world is getting to be so organised, if you take one breath per minute too many you get thrown in jail for using up other peoples air. Come on Crispin, what do you say? Come with me. Just come and see what it's like. If you don't like it you can always come back to… here.
CRISPIN:	What will I need? To bring I mean.
ANGELA:	As far as I'm concerned just bring yourself. But if you want to bring anything else, well that's up to you. As long as it isn't a snake. I don't think I could be doing with snakes.
CRISPIN:	I thought you said it was free.

ANGELA: Look, lets not brawl over it before we've even got out of this place. Let's just go, man. *(She gets up and holds out her hand)* Are you coming?

CRISPIN goes back to his pool.

You can share my mattress.

CRISPIN busily searches around for something.

I'll kick Jason out.

CRISPIN: *(Looking up)* Jason, who is Jason?

ANGELA: Oh, Jason is but the most beautiful person. He gives you a charge like no one I've ever known... yet.

CRISPIN: He won't be too pleased at my being there.

ANGELA: He'll be all right. Don't you worry?

CRISPIN: Oh, I'm not worried. Where is Jason now?

ANGELA: *(Shrugs)* We lost each other when we left the school. *(She gets down on her knees again beside CRISPIN)* Come with me, Crispin. Come with me.

He looks at her. The door opens, ALMA enters, stops dead at the sight of ANGELA's back and stands staring at the two young people on the floor. ANGELA leans forward for CRISPIN to kiss her. Instead he looks down and gently cups his hand over her breast. She opens her eyes to look at him, realising that his action is more a gesture to keep her at a distance.

ALMA: Crispin! Crispin, who or what is your friend?

CRISPIN: Her name is Angela and she came through the window.

ALMA: *(Looking at the window to visualise the scene)* I

	beg your pardon?
ANGELA:	*(Getting up)* I came through the window. I know Peter Pan is supposed to come to Wendy rather than the other way round, but in this case it was the other way round.
ALMA:	How long has she been here?
CRISPIN:	Quite a while.
ANGELA:	Quite a while.
ALMA:	And what is she doing here?
CRISPIN:	Talking to me.
ANGELA:	Talking to him.
ALMA:	And what has she been talking to you about?
ANGELA:	Look, I am here you know. You can talk to me. I'm not exactly invisible. If you want to ask me questions, ask away.
ALMA:	Crispin, why did she come through the window?
CRISPIN:	It was the only way she could find. She's hiding.
ALMA:	From what?
CRISPIN:	The police.
ANGELA:	The police.
ALMA:	*(Walking around to view ANGELA from another angle)* And you are harbouring her? A fugitive from justice? What has she done? Why is she in my house? She is part of the new permissive society you know I don't agree with the permissive society.

ANGELA: Crispin, are you coming with me?

ALMA: Come with you?

ANGELA: Oh! So I am here after all.

ALMA: Have you, a complete and total stranger, had the temerity to ask my son to go somewhere with you? Where to may I ask?

ANGELA: One may. Back to my place.

ALMA: Your place? Do you have a place? Wherever your place may be I am sure it is no place at all for Crispin.

ANGELA: This is no place for Crispin.

ALMA: Indeed. And why not? This is his home. Has always been his home. I am his mother. You are an intruder in this house and with respect, I must kindly ask you to leave at once.

ANGELA: Why?

ALMA: Because you have absolutely no right to be here.

ANGELA: I'm doing no harm.

ALMA: I have my doubts about that.

ANGELA: What if I refuse to go?

ALMA: Then, whatever it is you have, or have not done, and I do not wish to know about it, I shall be duty bound to call the police.

ANGELA: Crispin?

But CRISPIN has been blowing up the pool and is in no state to answer. ANGELA turns to ALMA.

	What if Crispin decides to come with me?
ALMA:	He won't. Anyway, why should you want him to go with you?
ANGELA:	Do I really have to answer that?
ALMA:	No, not really. Well I can tell you now and without any hesitation that you are not going to succeed with your siren song so you might as well trot this very instant.
ANGELA:	Crispin...

She goes back beside him just as DOLORES enters.

DOLORES:	I've left Fanny and Charlotte to clear away... *(She trails off and stares at ANGELA)* Who is that?
ALMA:	That is a friend of Crispin's. Her name is Angela and she came through the window.
DOLORES:	*(Looking at the window)* Through the window? Up the creeper?
ALMA:	And, it looks to me as though she sloughed her skin on the way up, poor creature.
DOLORES:	What is she doing here?
ALMA:	Endeavouring to persuade Crispin to run away with her.

DOLORES gasps and clutches her heart. She turns a look of horror on ANGELA.

DOLORES:	He's not going!
ALMA:	Of course not. The whole idea is preposterous.
ANGELA:	Why?

ALMA: Because, if you had any sense, you would realise you have nothing to offer him.

ANGELA: How do you know that? You know nothing about me.

ALMA: And I don't think we want to know anything about you either, young lady. But I do know my own child. Oh, Crispin, you've fixed the pool.

Under the pretext of examining CRISPIN's handiwork, but actually in order to be protectively closer, ALMA moves over to the pool. But CRISPIN picks it up and carries it to the centre of the room, narrowly missing both his mother and DOLORES on the way. They take avoiding action and CRISPIN drops the pool in the centre of the room and stands looking down at it.

CRISPIN: I don't think it will be big enough.

ALMA: I thought you said it was a baby alligator.

CRISPIN: And I don't know if that patch will hold.

ALMA: It will be perfectly all right in the basement. If it starts to go down the water will spill onto the stone floor.

CRISPIN: It can't go in the basement.

ALMA: Why not?

CRISPIN: It's too cold down there. The snakes are all right. They're in their vivariums. But the cold stone floor.

ALMA: Take an electric heater down. Take the sunlamp down.

CRISPIN: And what if Angela were to swish her tail and knock the heater into the pool? She'd be electrocuted.

DOLORES: Angela?

CRISPIN: That's her name. I named her after... *(Pointing)* ... this Angela here.

ALMA: Why?

CRISPIN: I don't know. It just seemed like a good idea.

ALMA: What are we going to do with him?

CRISPIN: Her. Angela is a her.

ALMA: YOU I'm talking about.

ANGELA: Why not leave him alone for a start?

ALMA: Did you say something?

DOLORES: I am sure the crocodile will be very comfortable in here.

ALMA: No!

DOLORES: *(Brightly)* In the garden then.

CRISPIN: She might get stolen. They're valuable creatures you know.

ALMA: Only to another crocodile.

CRISPIN: Alligator.

ALMA: All right, alligator.

DOLORES: It can't... I mean... it's only for two days, Alma. It can't do much harm just lying still in the swimming pool.

ALMA: There's no guarantee that it is just going to lie still in the swimming pool and I know of no household policy that covers damage by alligator. What if he

| | decides to take a walk? What if it messes on my carpet? What if it eats the curtains? |

CRISPIN: You're becoming confused with goats.

ANGELA: If you asked me it would be a good thing if it swished its tail and knocked the whole bloody house down.

ALMA: No one is asking you thank you very much. And, talking of walks, you haven't taken yours yet.

ANGELA: Do I really have to? I could become a friend of the family.

ALMA: Not in a thousand years. Go… and take the croco-alligator with you.

DOLORES: Alma!

She makes frantic signs meaning that, if ANGELA takes the croco-alligator with her, it will mean the departure of CRISPIN. It is while this semaphore is going on that CHARLOTTE enters.

CHARLOTTE: I've left Fanny doing the dishes. Hello, who is this?

DOLORES: Her name is Angela and she came through the window.

CHARLOTTE: *(Having taken a look at the window)* Through the window?

ALMA: Up the creeper and through the window.

CRISPIN: Over the garden wall up the creeper and through the window.

ANGELA: Down the street over the garden wall up the creeper and through the window.

CHARLOTTE: Rather a tortuous method of entry wasn't it?

CRISPIN:	She had no choice. There was nowhere downstairs she could get in.
ALMA:	Well, as luck and architecture would have it, there is somewhere downstairs she can get out. It's called a front door. If you go now we won't press charges.
DOLORES:	What charges?
ALMA:	Breaking and entering. Trespass. Soliciting for an immoral purpose.
CHARLOTTE:	Crispin?
ALMA:	Well I certainly hope not one of us.
CHARLOTTE:	*(Looking at him)* Crispin?
ALMA:	No one said anything about him responding did they?
CHARLOTTE:	Anyway *(Extending her hand)* I'm Charlotte, Crispin's sister.
ANGELA:	I know.
ALMA:	Do you?
ANGELA:	Yes, I was here when you all came in before.
CHARLOTTE:	*(Dropping her hand)* Were you? I didn't see you.
ANGELA:	I was hiding... behind that chair
ALMA:	Crispin? What have you been up to?
CRISPIN:	Nothing. I didn't ask her to choose this house to hide in. Did I? I never saw her before she came through that window.
ALMA:	Why didn't you come down and eat with us? And

                how is it she now wants you to go away with her?

CHARLOTTE: What?

DOLORES: She wants to take Crispin away from us.

CHARLOTTE: Why?

ANGELA: Because... Because... You're a bunch of cannibals that's why.

ALMA: *(Calmly)* What nonsense. And, if we were, what's it to you?

CHARLOTTE: Obviously she would like to be the one who's doing the eating.

ANGELA: That's not true. If he comes with me he will be free.

ALMA: And what is he now? He is his own master.

ANGELA: Is he?

ALMA: Of course he is. As much as any of us ever are. He's a grown boy. He can come and go as he pleases. Do as he pleases. Make up his own mind as he pleases.

ANGELA: Then why doesn't he please?

ALMA: He does. Don't you, darling?

ANGELA: He's IMPOTENT!

They all turn to look at her.

                He's... he's... *(Struggling for words)* He's castrated!

There is a shocked gasp from DOLORES. CHARLOTTE smiles. ALMA is icy. CRISPIN hurt.

CRISPIN: I am no such thing.

DOLORES:	I knew those snakes would cause trouble.
ALMA:	Charlotte, will you please go downstairs dear, and dial 999. Ask the police if they would be so kind as to come here and collect a piece of baggage. I knew it from the moment I clapped eyes on her, that she was one of those anything goes type of person. Run along, dear. The sooner it is done, the sooner this house can return to normal.
ANGELA:	Normal?
ALMA:	Normal is what normal is expected to be and, in this house it does not include you.

FANNY enters carrying the remains of a teapot. She marches straight into the room.

ANGELA:	That's about the lot, except for granny. All we need now is granny.
ALMA:	How dare you!
FANNY:	Please, madam is not to be angry with me… *(she holds out the spout)*… but the pour thing of the teapot I have broken.
ANGELA:	Don't let it worry you, girl that is not the only poor thing around here that seems to be broken.
ALMA:	Charlotte, are you going to call the police or do I have to do it?
FANNY:	Polizei! *(She looks around, bewildered)* Why are you to call the police, purlease?
ANGELA:	Relax, relax, I am the criminal element here, not you. My name is Angela and I came through the window.

FANNY turns to look at the window.

                        Down the street, over the garden wall, up the creeper and through the window. I tell you all this before you ask and before they have to tell you. And now I want to go out again and take Crispin with me. Yes, just as much as you want to take him to Germany.

DOLORES:
ALMA: What!
CHARLOTTE:

ANGELA: But they won't let me.

ALMA: Fanny? What is this she says?

DOLORES: Take Crispin to Germany?

FANNY: Why not, please?

DOLORES: Never Germany!

ALMA: Fanny, you have been trusted in this house.

FANNY: That is right.

ALMA: And you betrayed that trust, getting at my son, behind our backs.

DOLORES: I knew all along a German could not be trusted. Did I not tell you so?

CHARLOTTE: You told me so.

ALMA: I shall have to seriously consider sending you back home, Fanny.

FANNY: What about the teapot?

ALMA: Stuff the teapot!

FANNY: I don't understand. What does it mean please to

	stuff the teapot?
ALMA:	You are the cause of all this.
ANGELA:	No, you are *(to DOLORES)* and you *(CHARLOTTE)* and you.
ALMA:	And tonight of all nights when we've got tomorrow to face up to.
DOLORES:	There's not enough respect in the world these days.
ANGELA:	And is that such a bad thing?
ALMA:	Yes it is.
FANNY:	Mein gott, die sind alle verrückt! *(My god, they are all mad)*
CHARLOTTE:	Halts maul! *(Shut your hole!)*

FANNY gasps and hurls down the teapot.

CRISPIN:	Oh, shut up, all of you!

They all shut up.

Listen

There is the sound of a musical whistle.

ALMA:	What is it?
ANGELA:	It's Jason.

The whistle is repeated. ANGELA answers with her own whistle.

Good night.

She walks to the door and goes out immediately comes back and stands in the doorway, surveying them all.

                    Whatever happened to his father?

ALMA: That is private and confidential and no concern of yours.

The whistle from outside is repeated.

ANGELA: Crispin?

CRISPIN: He's dead.

ANGELA: Pity. I can't help feeling, if things had been just slightly different, I would have snapped him up from under your feet like a sparrow pecking up a crumb.

The whistle is repeated.

                    If you should change your mind Crispin, you know where to find me.

ANGELA goes out. They stand looking at the closed door for a moment as though expecting it to open again but it doesn't. CRISPIN crouches by the swimming pool and from it takes the remains of the teapot. He stands and holds the pool.

CRISPIN: She's punctured the swimming pool.

There is the hiss of air escaping and the pool deflates as the curtain comes down.

Act Three

FANNY, CHARLOTTE, DOLORES, ALMA and CRISPIN exactly as we left them, all looking at the pool which is now flat. DOLORES glances at the door.

DOLORES: That dreadful creature. I do hope she doesn't disturb granny on the way out.

CHARLOTTE: How, may one ask, is she likely to disturb granny?

DOLORES: Don't you think someone ought to see her safely off these premises? What a shocking condition she's in. If that is the result of the welfare state then, all I can say is, the sooner we get rid of the welfare state the better. If that's all the appreciation one gets for paying exorbitant taxes to help towards their upbringing, updragging rather...

ALMA: Oh, for goodness sake, Dolores, don't go on. The girl is a complete, to use the vulgar American expression, a complete phoney. She fondly imagines that if she pads barefoot down the Kings road looking like a cross between an Indian squaw and a Victorian laundry basket and picking up a few transatlantic expressions on the way she has somehow solved the riddle of life. She'll get over it.

DOLORES: Maybe. But will we? Climbing into peoples houses without so much as a by your leave. And the insults! You were much too patient with her, Alma. The way she was getting at Crispin.

CRISPIN stoops and retrieves the pieces of the teapot from the pool. He passes them to DOLORES who passes them to CHARLOTTE who passes them to FANNY.

I haven't heard the front door bang. Do you think she's gone out? Maybe someone ought to go and look. She could be doing... things... downstairs.

CHARLOTTE: You can't hear the front door from here, unless it's taken off its hinges and thrown.

DOLORES: Well, maybe she's left it wide open. She could come back with all her cronies.

ALMA: Oh, Dolores, please!

DOLORES: I only hope she hasn't interfered with granny.

ALMA: Dolores, I think you had better take some aspirin and go to bed.

DOLORES: I'd never be able to sleep.

ALMA: Then go downstairs and check the front door but don't merely stand there talking about it.

CRISPIN: *(Who has been examining the pool)* There's no chance whatsoever of me repairing that. There aren't enough patches for a start. She'll just have to stay in the bath until I can think of something.

ALMA: The scullery sink.

CRISPIN: *(Shakes his head)* No, I'll think of something.

CHARLOTTE: How dirty do we have to be before you do?

DOLORES: Oh, Crispin, why can't you keep harmless pets like... Rabbits? Little furry creatures. Cuddly creatures. Or hamsters.

CRISPIN: Hamsters are vicious. They bite.

ALMA:	They don't need bathtubs of water which is something to be said in there favour.
CRISPIN:	I know! Isn't there an old tarpaulin somewhere? Maybe I could fix it up. Hold up the corners with some rope or something.
ALMA:	It's in the coal shed. And there's some rope in the pantry. Fanny, did you finish doing the dishes?
FANNY:	No. I came to tell you how I have broken the teapot.
ALMA:	Well never mind the teapot. Go and finish cleaning up downstairs, dear. Charlotte go and help her. I could never abide a dirty kitchen.

FANNY goes.

CHARLOTTE:	Crispin, you won't forget the designs will you?
ALMA:	What designs?
CHARLOTTE:	Only some I brought home. Don't sound so suspicious mother.
ALMA:	After all the goings on this evening I have every right to sound suspicious.
CHARLOTTE:	All I want is for Crispin to take a look at them and give me his opinion. He is going no further than my room.
DOLORES:	What are they, dear?

DOLORES bites her lip and throws a quick, guilty glance at ALMA but ALMA doesn't seem to notice.

ALMA:	All right, but go and help Fanny first.
CHARLOTTE:	*(Going)* Won't be long. *(At the door)* If you want a hand with your tarpaulin, Crispin, just yell.

She goes out.

ALMA: What about you, Dolores? What do you propose to do?

DOLORES: I think I'll take your advice dear and go to bed with a couple of aspirins. It really has been the most trying day. Of course I shouldn't really have been expected to work today at all... *(Making for the door)*... but we are so shorthanded, what with the holiday rota, and there's an epidemic of hepatitis going around at the moment. There also have been some permanent departures. People seem to have no idea of responsibility these days, no idea at all. And replacing them is like trying to find the proverbial needle in a haystack. *(For CRISPINS benefit)* It is impossible to find the right kind, the right sort of person. No one takes any pride anymore, in what they do. Is it any wonder the country's in the state it's in? You won't stay up too late will you, dear? We've got such a day tomorrow.

ALMA: I won't be long out of bed.

DOLORES: You too, Crispin, don't sit down here all night, there's a good boy.

CRISPIN: I have to fix up a pool for Angela first.

DOLORES: And don't go to bed on an empty stomach.

ALMA: Dolores...

DOLORES: Your food is in the oven. You really oughtn't to be so careless with your meals.

ALMA: Dolores, if you carry on talking, it will be breakfast time before you reach the top of the stairs.

DOLORES: I was only thinking of Crispin. He needs his

	strength.
ALMA:	So do I.
DOLORES:	Yes... well... have I forgotten anything? *(She looks around the room)* No. I'll say good night then.
ALMA:	Good night.
DOLORES:	Though how a body is expected to sleep after...
ALMA:	Dolores.
DOLORES:	Yes, good night, Crispin.
CRISPIN:	Good night aunt.
DOLORES:	I'm sorry you don't like your shirt.

And before anyone can contradict her, she is gone. ALMA heaves a sigh of relief and switches on a table lamp. She looks up to see CRISPIN smiling at her.

ALMA:	What are you laughing at?
CRISPIN:	I'm not laughing, I'm smiling
ALMA:	Oh.

She switches on another lamp.

CRISPIN:	You order everyone to change for dinner and you're still walking around like that.
ALMA:	It would be a rather silly gesture to change it now only to change again for bed. You bought it for me.
CRISPIN:	I know.
ALMA:	Last birthday. You have impeccable taste in clothes, Crispin.

CRISPIN:	Yes.
ALMA:	Do you know what I think?
CRISPIN:	Tell me.
ALMA:	I think, once we've got tomorrow out of the way, you and I will go on a shopping expedition.
CRISPIN:	All right.
ALMA:	And I'll leave all the choosing up to you. Every bit of it.

CRISPIN nods and throws down the pool.

	Is there really no chance of repairing that?
CRISPIN:	No chance at all. It's beyond hope. Does Angela really have to go back to Harrods?
ALMA:	We'll see. *(She puts her arms over his shoulders)* It's nice... isn't it?
CRISPIN:	What is?
ALMA:	The fact that we're such good friends.
CRISPIN:	Yes.
ALMA:	We are good friends aren't we?
CRISPIN:	Of course. *(He kisses her lightly)*
ALMA:	My beautiful son. *(Holds his face in her hands)* Do I really have you all to myself for a few precious moments?
CRISPIN:	You've had me... *(Removing her hands so that he can talk)* You've had me to yourself all day.

ALMA:	No I haven't. I've had to share you with a lot of beastly snakes. And, had I but known it, an alligator.
CRISPIN:	I'm quite prepared to share the beastly snakes with you.
ALMA:	You weren't really interested in going with that girl were you?
CRISPIN:	No.
ALMA:	No, I didn't think you would be. I only wanted to make sure.
CRISPIN:	Why? Would it have worried you if I had?
ALMA:	Of course it would. She's not the type of girl for you. Did she… did she make… suggestions?
CRISPIN:	What sort of suggestions?
ALMA:	Oh, Crispin! Don't pretend to be so naïve.
CRISPIN:	No, she didn't make any suggestions.

ALMA is mightily relieved.

	She made an out right proposition.
ALMA:	What!
CRISPIN:	Yes, she asked me to share her mattress.
ALMA:	At your very first meeting? It was your very first meeting wasn't it?
CRISPIN:	Yes.
ALMA:	Life really does move fast these days. Share her mattress. Doesn't she even have a bed? No I suppose not, there hasn't been time to get one. My

	God, what are the youth of today coming to?
CRISPIN:	Well at least she didn't ask me to share a bush in Hyde Park.
ALMA:	Why, has someone asked you to? And what's all this about Fanny asking you to go to Germany?
CRISPIN:	She wants me to go and stay with her family.
ALMA:	Has she asked them?
CRISPIN:	Evidently. And they said they would be delighted to have me.
ALMA:	I'm sure they would. Well, Fanny might have had the courtesy to ask me first.
CRISPIN:	Why?
ALMA:	She asked HER family for approval didn't she?
CRISPIN:	That's different.
ALMA:	No difference at all. Don't argue with me, Crispin.
CRISPIN:	Mother, tell me about my father.
ALMA:	Why?
CRISPIN:	I want you to talk about him. You never do. I want to hear you talk about him.
ALMA:	Not tonight, Crispin, some other time maybe.
CRISPIN:	No, now. I want to hear you talk about him now.
ALMA:	No, Crispin, I'm distressed enough as it is this evening. We must comfort each other not cause distress.
CRISPIN:	I know granny never liked him.

ALMA: Crispin.

CRISPIN: Never approved of him. She told me so. Did you never think of marrying again? You could have done. You could still. You're very beautiful. A lot of men would...

ALMA: Crispin! I do not want to discuss either your father or my personal emotional life either. I won't hear another word.

CRISPIN: We don't have to get emotional over it. We can sit here quite calmly, the two of us, and talk quietly, in whispers if you like. What is there to hide? People don't get on with each other. They find out they've made a mistake and...

ALMA: Oh... *(She clutches her forehead)* You've brought on one of my headaches. I asked you not to talk about... I ... you know how it distresses me. I'm not ashamed, or hiding anything. I just don't remember.

CRISPIN: But you must remember. Every time you look at me you must remember.

ALMA: Please, Crispin...

She makes for the door.

CRISPIN: Where are you going?

But ALMA doesn't even turn around.

Mother come back. I didn't mean to... Mother?

CRISPIN flops into the sofa. He sits for a moment, frowning, then stretches out his legs and looks at his feet. Then he looks at his hands, front and back. He tenses his legs, lifting his feet off the floor, and prods his thigh muscles. He runs his hands up his thighs feeling the curve of the muscles then, opening his shirt, he prods his stomach before rubbing his hand upwards from his navel to his neck. He is examining his torso with interest when a figure enters through the window. This is JASON, the male counterpart of ANGELA. He is wearing a pair of tight, tattered and stained jeans and brightly coloured waistcoat. His arms and chest are bare except for ornaments and his hair flows down his shoulders. He is about to advance into the room when the door opens and CHARLOTTE enters. JASON retreats onto the balcony.

CHARLOTTE: Crispin?

CRISPIN: Yes?

CHARLOTTE: What are you doing?

CRISPIN: Looking at myself.

CHARLOTTE: What for?

CRISPIN: I was interested.

CHARLOTTE: *(Leaning over the back of the sofa, and rubbing his chest)* What about the designs?

CRISPIN: *(Dropping his head back to look up at her)* What about them?

CHARLOTTE: Now?

CRISPIN: I have to do Angela's pool first.

JASON, who is half way to swinging his leg over the balcony reacts to the name.

CHARLOTTE: Oh, Crispin, you promised.

CRISPIN: I promised, and I'll keep my promise. But you wanted to take a bath didn't you? And I also promised to fix up Angela.

CHARLOTTE: *(Putting her head next to his)* One of these days,

	sweet brother, someone is not going to let you have it all your own way. Someone is going to see right through you. And what will you do then.
CRISPIN:	I don't know. I'll have to wait till it happens to find out.

CHARLOTTE laughs, kisses his cheek, and moves away. JASON is now behind the curtain.

CHARLOTTE:	Where's mother?
CRISPIN:	I think she went upstairs. Aunt Dolores has gone to bed. At least that's where she said she was going.
CHARLOTTE:	Do you want some help with the tarpaulin?
CRISPIN:	No.
CHARLOTTE:	*(Moving back to him)* You won't be too long will you?

CRISPIN shakes his head.

	I want to do some more work on the drawings anyway so come up when you've finished.

CRISPIN nods. CHARLOTTE gives his shoulder a squeeze and heads for the door.

CRISPIN:	What have you done with Fanny?
CHARLOTTE:	Buried her.
CRISPIN:	That's not a very nice thing to say. Seriously.
CHARLOTTE:	Metaphorically speaking she is buried under a pile of ironing in the kitchen, mostly yours I believe. She insisted on doing it. I think she wants to work something out of her system. Have you...?
CRISPIN:	*(Looks at CHARLOTTE, looks down again)* I

	don't think that's quite the sort of question a sister should ask, or even think about.
CHARLOTTE:	I don't suppose it's of any consequence anyway, unless...

She shrugs and goes out. CRISPIN goes back to the study of his body and JASON once more enters the room. He gives a whistle, very softly, and CRISPIN looks up. CRISPIN turns and sees JASON. For a moment they regard each other and then CRISPIN gets off the sofa and moves over to JASON.

CRISPIN:	Jason?
JASON:	*(Nods and looks around)* Where's Angie?
CRISPIN:	She's not here. She left. She heard you whistle and she went out – that way.
JASON:	I didn't see her. I thought her whistle came from up here so I waited. But, when she didn't show up, I hopped over the wall to come and look for her. You said something about fixing her up.
CRISPIN:	Oh, no, that's not your Angela. That's my Angela.
JASON:	You have an Angela too? Well what happened to my Angela. Where is she, baby?
CRISPIN:	*(Shrugs)* By the time she got round to the wall where you were waiting, you were already over it and looking for her.
JASON:	So instead of finding her I find you. What was she doing here, anyway?
CRISPIN:	She was hiding. Weren't you?
JASON:	Jason doesn't hide, baby.
CRISPIN:	What were you doing then.

JASON: If you really want to know I was having a piss. In a public convenience.

CRISPIN: That was convenient.

JASON chooses to ignore this.

JASON: I don't dig this place, baby.

CRISPIN: Would you like a drink?

JASON: *(Shakes his head)* No. *(After another look around)* Well, suppose I might as well find out what's happened to her. *(He heads for the window)* I've got nothing better to do.

CRISPIN: You mean you're leaving?

JASON: That's the general idea. Is there a reason why I shouldn't? *(He reaches the window)* I'll tell Angie I saw you. *(Turning)* What's your name?

CRISPIN: Crispin.

JASON: *(Smiling)* Well... Crispin...

He nods, turns back to the window.

CRISPIN: Are you really going to look for her?

JASON: If it turns out a drag I can wait for her back at the pad. She'll turn up sooner or later.

CRISPIN: When you find her...

JASON stops and turns back.

Tell her... tell her I've been thinking about what she said and I might take her up on it.

JASON pretends to think for a moment and the nods.

JASON: *(Seriously)* Okay, Crispin, I'll tell her.

Once more he turns back to the window.

CRISPIN: Don't you even want to know what it was? What she said?

JASON: Crispin, you're a gas, baby, do you know that?

CRISPIN: Am I?

JASON: Hey, do you want to come back with me now and wait for her?

CRISPIN: Jason you don't understand.

JASON: Oh, I understand all right.

CRISPIN: She asked me to come and live with her.

JASON: Yeah, I know.

CRISPIN: And you don't mind?

JASON: She's no special chick. And she's a big girl now. She knows what she wants.

CRISPIN: She said she'd kick you out.

JASON: Did she so?

CRISPIN: To make room for me.

JASON: She doesn't have to do that. There's plenty of room for you. Still, if that's what she wants. I mean, she's done it before, and before, and before. It's no new scene, baby. I can go my own way. *(He sees CRISPIN's serious face and laughs)* Oh, don't let it bring you down, baby. If you want to make it with Angie that's Okay. But, whatever you do, like don't take Angie for real, man *(He puts out a hand and taking CRISPIN gently by the side of*

	the neck shakes him) Keep your cool, baby. It's the only way. See you.
CRISPIN:	*(Grabbing the hand)* If you aren't really anxious to find her why do you have to go?
JASON:	You mean you don't want me to?
CRISPIN:	No. Yes. I mean no, I don't want you to.
JASON:	*(Thinks about it)* Okay. Can I have my hand back now?
CRISPIN:	Oh, yes. I'm sorry.
JASON:	No need. I mean, if you want to keep it, keep it. So long as it makes you happy. *(He moves back into the room)* Okay, so what are we going to do?
CRISPIN:	Are you hungry? There's some food in the oven.
JASON:	No, I'm not hungry.
CRISPIN:	Angela was.
JASON:	Angela always is. I've never known Angela when she wasn't. And that goes for pretty boys too. Hey, didn't you say, correct me if I'm wrong, that you had an Angela of your own?
CRISPIN:	Yes.
JASON:	Was that her in here with you a few minutes ago?
CRISPIN:	No, that was my sister, Charlotte. The other Angela, well… she's not human.
JASON:	Then what is she?
CRISPIN:	An alligator.
JASON:	A stuffed one?

CRISPIN: No, a live one. She's in the bath at the moment.

JASON: Can I take a look at this alligator in the bath?

CRISPIN: Do you want to?

JASON: Jason, doesn't say anything he doesn't mean, baby. If Jason says he wants to take a look at an alligator in the bath that's exactly what Jason wants to do. The time for beating around the bush died a hundred years ago. Maybe people haven't caught on to the idea yet but that's how it is now. Now you turn me on, Crispin, and I don't mind saying so. I don't know all the reasons but one of them is I like the idea of a guy who keeps an alligator in his bath, so lead me to the tub and the Lady Angela.

CRISPIN: Right. Would you do me a favour and help me carry her downstairs?

JASON: For you, baby, anything.

CRISPIN: I have to get her down to the basement you see. I keep the snakes down there.

JASON: Snakes? You keep snakes in the basement?

CRISPIN: Yes. Two constrictors, a python and a horned viper.

JASON: Crazy. Well come on and let's take a look.

CRISPIN: Do you know, you are the first person who has ever come into this house who actually wanted to look at my snakes. I mean, you didn't even wait to be asked. You asked me.

JASON: In your book that makes me something special?

CRISPIN stands staring at JASON in obvious admiration. Then he picks up the shirt still in its wrapping and thrusts it towards his visitor.

	What's this?
CRISPIN:	It's a shirt.
JASON:	What're you giving it to me for? Do I look as if I want a shirt?
CRISPIN:	I want you to have it.
JASON:	Okay, if it makes you happy.

He slips off his waistcoat and hands it to CRISPIN, takes the shirt out and holds it up.

| CRISPIN: | Watch out for pins. New shirts have more pins than a cushion. Here, I'll help you. |

They start pulling pins out.

JASON:	You sure? Is she a peace loving alligator?
CRISPIN:	I'll take the mouth. I know how to handle her. You can take the tail.
JASON:	I know how to handle that?

He puts the pins in a convenient ashtray as JASON puts on the shirt.

| | I'll leave the tail out. I don't think it'll fit in my pants. |
| CRISPIN: | *(Handing back the waistcoat)* Ready? This way. |

CRISPIN is about to open the door when he hears something, turns back and puts his finger to his lips, pushing JASON into the corner behind the door and the two of them squeeze up against the wall as the door opens and ALMA looks in.

| ALMA: | Crispin? |

She enters and looks around, sees the open window and crosses to close it. CRISPIN takes JASON by the hand and they slip out of the room. ALMA, having closed the window, takes a cigarette from a box and lights it. Then she notices the cellophane on the floor and the pins in the ashtray. She picks up the cellophane and is standing with it in her hand when CHARLOTTE enters.

CHARLOTTE: Where's Crispin?

ALMA: I have absolutely no idea where Crispin is. Probably in the basement with his snakes.

CHARLOTTE: He said he was going to see to the tarpaulin.

ALMA: Then that is probably what he is doing. Has he removed that... thing... from the bathtub yet?

CHARLOTTE: I don't know, I haven't looked. I've been upstairs drawing.

ALMA: You could have looked on the way down.

CHARLOTTE: I've given up all hopes, plans, and ambitions of having a bath tonight, mother dear, I shall go to bed dirty.

ALMA: He might have taken it out... though why he has to put on his new shirt to do it I really have no idea. Unless... *(She looks towards the window and shakes her head, refusing to believe It. Screws up the cellophane and drops it)* Pity about the swimming pool. We could have used it this summer.

CHARLOTTE: For what? We haven't used it for years. It's much too small.

ALMA: If we haven't used it for years then how come it had an arrow shot through it last summer?

CHARLOTTE: Crispin thought it would make a good target stand.

ALMA: Target stand?

CHARLOTTE: Yes, standing on edge.

ALMA: What a ridiculous idea. I've a jolly good mind to make him buy a new one.

CHARLOTTE: What have you two been fighting about?

ALMA: Fighting? Who said anything about fighting?

CHARLOTTE: You did. From the moment I walked into the room.

ALMA: We haven't had a fight. Crispin and I have never had a fight in the whole of his life.

CHARLOTTE: Then why are you in such a mood?

ALMA stubs out her cigarette.

               Only Crispin can put you in such a mood.

ALMA: He wanted to talk about his father.

CHARLOTTE: His father?

ALMA: His father, your father. He wanted me to talk about him and I refused. He insisted upon going on even when I begged him not to. But we did not have a fight. It brought on one of my headaches that's all.

CHARLOTTE: Better now?

ALMA: No. Anyway, I came down to make it up.

CHARLOTTE: The fight you didn't have.

ALMA: I came down to explain about the headache.

CHARLOTTE: He knows you are under a strain.

ALMA: What strain? There's no strain. It's a great and blessed relief. You know that as much as I do. Dolores is the one who is making the melodrama out of it. Dolores could make a melodrama out of crumpets and honey for high tea. Did Crispin eat his dinner do you know?

CHARLOTTE: I don't think so.

ALMA: He must be starving. I wonder if he would take a snack.

CHARLOTTE: If his nose is wet he might.

ALMA: And where is Fanny?

CHARLOTTE: The last I saw of her she was in the kitchen ironing his underpants.

ALMA: You don't iron underpants.

CHARLOTTE: Fanny does. Nylon ones.

ALMA: That girl has got to go. This is really getting serious. Charlotte, you don't suppose he might have gone out. What if he's gone after that girl? Didn't she say he'd know where to find her?

CHARLOTTE: She did.

ALMA: Do you think he might have gone to her? Oh, my poor baby, I hope not. Imagine that for a daughter in law.

CHARLOTTE: Now who is being melodramatic? Who said anything about marriage? I should think that is as far from her mind as it is from his. Bed yes, marriage no. They'll probably give each others flowers, light candles and incense and read poetry.

ALMA: Poetry? That obscene stuff from San Francisco. That's not poetry. That's filth.

CHARLOTTE: How do you know?

ALMA: I saw some – on a shelf in a bookshop the other day. Really Charlotte, if you see 'Poetry' printed on the cover of a book you don't expect to open it and have four letter words leap out at you on motor cycles, do you?

CHARLOTTE laughs

I don't see that it's any laughing matter.

CHARLOTTE: What bookshop was it?

ALMA: Oh, have no fear, it was perfectly respectable. Or supposed to be.

CHARLOTTE: Do they sell your books there?

ALMA: They do.

CHARLOTTE: Then why don't you tell your publishers to put an embargo on them? Have your books withdrawn as a protest. After all you can't send a gunboat up the aisle between economic theory on your left and political history on your right so try sanctions. Every one else seems to be trying it. You may be more successful. And think of the moral pat on the back you could give yourself.

ALMA: I really do not know, Charlotte, how you ever came to be my daughter.

CHARLOTTE: Don't you? Well, that's news. Were you waiting till I was grown up enough to tell me?

ALMA: Sometimes you talk such arrant nonsense, I really do think you must be a changeling.

CHARLOTTE: Why? Was there a fairy at the bottom of the garden?

ALMA: That is not funny.

CHARLOTTE: Many a true word as they say. It was only a shot in the dark. That was an unfortunate turn of phrase.

ALMA: There you go again. Such rubbish.

CHARLOTTE: No more, mother dear, than your silly books.

ALMA: Charlotte! You don't mean that.

CHARLOTTE: All right, I didn't mean it.

ALMA: No, but you did.

CHARLOTTE: Mother, make up your mind, either I did or I didn't.

ALMA: It doesn't matter. Whatever your opinion may be, my books have fed, clothed, and housed you for most of your natural life.

CHARLOTTE: Surprising really, considering how cheap they are, in price I mean.

ALMA: They're popular. And they are popular because they are good of their kind. That is what matters, for something to be good of its kind. Comparisons are odious especially where there is no similitude in what is being compared.

CHARLOTTE: Surprising then that you should do it so often.

ALMA: I never do. When do I ever make comparisons?

CHARLOTTE: I suppose all parents do it really, though I would have though you'd notice by now that your two do happen to be one of each sex.

ALMA: You're talking nonsense again. And if all parents make comparisons then all children are jealous of each other so don't think you're anything out of the ordinary, my girl.

CHARLOTTE: You don't know what I'm talking about do you?

ALMA: Neither do you so there's an end to it. You've hurt me deeply. Saying such mean things about my work. Crispin would nev... Yes, well... Charlotte, be a dear and see if you can find him. He must be around somewhere.

CHARLOTTE: Why don't you try the basement?

ALMA: What?

CHARLOTTE: You don't have to go in. Knock on the door.

ALMA: He could be in there and chose not to answer. So I would be none the wiser would I? And you are the one who wants him.

CHARLOTTE: Am I?

ALMA: To look at your drawings.

CHARLOTTE: Hmn... well, they can wait. I'm not going to work tomorrow anyway.

ALMA: He won't want to look at them tomorrow.

CHARLOTTE: Why not?

ALMA: He won't be in any state. Charlotte, you know how sensitive he is. Tomorrow is going to be very hard on all of us, just having to go through with it.

CHARLOTTE: If the last couple of days haven't been hard then I don't see why tomorrow should be any worse.

ALMA: You don't understand, dear. On the surface all

might appear to be normal but this sort of thing must have an affect below the surface. It's bound to, isn't it? We might even appear to be glad but really that is only a defence mechanism.

The door opens and DOLORES looks in.

ALMA: Now what are you doing here? You're supposed to be in bed.

DOLORES: I couldn't find any aspirin.

ALMA: In the bathroom. In the medicine chest.

DOLORES: I'm not going in there.

ALMA: Then you'll have to go to bed aspirin less.

DOLORES: Haven't you got any?

ALMA: No.

DOLORES: Charlotte?

CHARLOTTE shakes her head.

Oh, dear, I'm never going to get through tomorrow. I simply won't be able to face it I know I won't. *(Suddenly noticing)* Where's Crispin?

ALMA: Neither of us has the slightest idea.

DOLORES: Maybe he's gone to bed.

ALMA: Which is where you should be? Good night, Dolores.

DOLORES: Yes. Good night.

She goes out, closing the door.

ALMA: It's a truly great pity that sister of mine never got

	married. I wish someone would provide me with a defence mechanism against her. I'm going to have her on my bones for the rest of my life I know.
CHARLOTTE:	One day you may be grateful for that.
ALMA:	Why?
CHARLOTTE:	Well has it never occurred to you, mother dear, that one day the fledglings will discover their wings and fly the nest? I should think that Aunt Dolores's company would be preferable to no company at all.
ALMA:	Has Crispin said anything to you about leaving? Has he been talking to you? No, I'm sure he hasn't. He would come to me first. Crispin's never done anything without discussing it with me. He has no secrets from me.
CHARLOTTE:	Mother, you had better start getting used to the idea now that sometime, we... you are going to lose him. No matter how hard you try to prevent it.
ALMA:	I'll never lose him, never. He'll always be my son no matter where he is or what he is doing. Why are you talking like this? Has something happened that I don't know about?
CHARLOTTE:	I merely state the obvious.
ALMA:	It isn't obvious to me.
CHARLOTTE:	That's why I'm stating it.

The door opens and FANNY peeps in, sees ALMA and immediately closes the door again but ALMA has seen her.

ALMA:	Fanny?

The door opens again and FANNY's head appears.

	Have you finished ironing?
FANNY:	Yes.
ALMA:	Then come in here for a moment, I want to talk to you.

FANNY considers and then reluctantly enters the room.

	Charlotte, haven't you got things to do? Drawings and things?
CHARLOTTE:	Why? Do you want me to go?

ALMA represses a reply and glares at her daughter.

	(Laughing) All right. *(To FANNY)* I advise you to plead guilty; it'll go easier for you.

She starts to go but, before she can move, there is a scream from upstairs.

ALMA:	Oh, my god! Not again? What now?

The scream is repeated, a little nearer.

FANNY:	Scheisse und schmutziges leben!

They all turn towards the door and wait for DOLORES to burst in which she does as dramatically as she can manage.

DOLORES:	There's... there's... a man in Crispin's room. A strange man. At least I think it's a man. Yes, I'm sure it is. And he's wearing Crispin's shirt!
ALMA:	What were you doing in Crispin's room?
DOLORES:	I went to see if he had any aspirin.
ALMA:	Is he there?

DOLORES: I don't know. I didn't wait to see. I took one look at that... creature... and fled. My heart is still pumping.

CHARLOTTE: I should hope so.

DOLORES: I can feel it. *(Looking down)* I can see it!

She staggers to a seat as ALMA opens the door and shouts.

ALMA: Crispin? Crispin! Come down here. I want to speak to you. And bring down whoever it is who's with you. *(She turns back)* What is happening in this house tonight?

DOLORES: That is what I would like to know.

ALMA: Did anyone hear the door bell ring?

FANNY: I hear nothing in the kitchen because the radio is turned up.

DOLORES: I didn't hear it. But then, as my room is right at the very top of the house...

ALMA heaves a very audible sigh which cuts DOLORES short.

ALMA: The house is suddenly bursting at the seems with the oddest creatures.

DOLORES: And nothing could be more odd that that creature up there. I can't tell you the fright it gave me.

ALMA: You can, and no doubt will, at great length.

CHARLOTTE: And greater length and greater length.

ALMA: Charlotte! That's enough. Kindly have a little more respect for your elders. If you've got nothing better to do then go back to your drawings.

DOLORES: No! Oughtn't we to stay together? I mean, with

	strange creatures on the loose in the house you never know what they might be up to. We don't even know what he's doing here. Oh, I do hope Crispin is all right.
CRISPIN:	Crispin is all right.

They all turn to the doorway where CRISPIN is standing. He has changed clothes with JASON and there is a long silence as the women take in the waistcoat, the beads, etc. Alma finally finds something her voice.

ALMA:	Crispin... what... where?... Crispin...?

CRISPIN enters the room followed by JASON. DOLORES moves into a position of comparative safety behind ALMA.

DOLORES:	You see? What did I tell you? He's wearing Crispin's shirt. The shirt I gave him.
CHARLOTTE:	What is Crispin wearing?
ALMA:	Somebody is going to have to do some explaining. Now just what is going on? Crispin, who is this?
CRISPIN:	This is Jason.
ALMA:	And who is Jason?
JASON:	I am Jason.
ALMA:	And where did Jason come from? I suppose he came through the window as well.
JASON:	That's right.
DOLORES:	What!
JASON:	I came through the window.
ALMA:	*(Almost hysterical)* Look, young man, who are you and what are you doing here?

JASON: Well...

ALMA: *(All in one breathe)* Don't prevaricate. Answer me. Crispin what are you doing in those ridiculous clothes? You'll catch something. I insist this young man leaves this house this very instant.

CRISPIN: That's all right mother, we're just going.

ALMA: Good.

Pause.

CHARLOTTE: Mother.

ALMA: Now please don't interfere, Charlotte.

CHARLOTTE: You didn't hear what my brother said.

ALMA: I heard, I heard. *(Suddenly suspicious)* What did he say?

CHARLOTTE: Repeat it for mother, Crispin.

CRISPIN: I said we're just going.

ALMA: We? We?

CRISPIN: Yes, I'm going with Jason.

ALMA: Where to?

CRISPIN: Back to his place.

ALMA: Where is that?

CRISPIN: Same place as Angela's.

ALMA: Now?

DOLORES: Oh, Crispin, You can't.

ALMA: Now?

CRISPIN nods happily.

What for?

CRISPIN: Because I want to.

ALMA: What are you talking about? Did you know this... *(Waving a hand in Jason's direction)* ...this creature before he slid through the window?

CRISPIN: No.

ALMA: Then it's a very sudden decision, isn't it?

JASON: That's how decisions should be, man.

ALMA: I am his mother, not his father. And you keep out of this. I am discussing something with my son.

JASON: Decisions should be taken on the spur of the moment, on an impulse. That way they'll be the right ones. Everything in its season, ma. There's a time for reaping and a time for sowing.

ALMA: Don't you quote the Scriptures at me you... you... pagan!

JASON: A time for coming and a time for going. Now is the time for Crispin to go. Come on, baby.

Standing behind CRISPIN, he puts his arm over CRISPIN's shoulder so that his hand and forearm are flat against CRISPIN's chest.

ALMA: Take your hand off my son.

JASON: Why? Is he delicate? Is he fragile? Will he break up and fall apart? I have a gentle touch, strong but gentle.

DOLORES: Alma, what are we going to do?

JASON: Do you want me to take my hands off you, baby?

CRISPIN shakes his head.

ALMA: So you're going.

CRISPIN nods

When will you be back?

CRISPIN: I don't know. We'll see.

ALMA: You mean you're not coming back tonight?

JASON: That's the general idea.

DOLORES: Oh, Crispin!

DOLORES takes out her handkerchief as she starts to weep – not too much – she still has to concentrate on the proceedings

ALMA: I don't understand it. I do not understand it. You're making a very grave mistake, Crispin. I mean, after all, this is your home, darling. This is where you belong, where you were brought up. This is where your memories are. How can you just up stakes and leave at a moment's notice? Haven't we been wonderfully happy here? Haven't we given you everything your heart could want? Why do you have to leave us? I tell you what. Think about it. Don't go until you've had a good think about it. Have your dinner. I'm sure Jason is hungry, I'll rustle him up something. You don't have to go yet.

FANNY: You can come to Germany, Crispin. Germany is very good for thinking.

ALMA: He is not going to Germany. Don't confuse the issue. Crispin, for our sakes, your family, please

	think about it.
CRISPIN:	I have thought about it. I want to go with Jason.
ALMA:	Then you couldn't have thought about it very clearly. What about the effect on us? What about your snakes? What about your alligator?
CRISPIN:	Phone up the zoo, ask them to come around and collect.
CHARLOTTE:	I don't believe it.
CRISPIN:	Why? The zoo will be very happy to have them.
ALMA:	What about all the things you'll need?
JASON:	What does he need?
ALMA:	What about money?
JASON:	Bread is no problem.
CRISPIN:	Right, we'll be off then. Okay, Jason?
JASON:	I'm right with you.
ALMA:	Crispin!

CRISPIN, who has turned to the door, turns back again.

DOLORES:	Listen to your mother, Crispin. A boy's best friend is his mother.
ALMA:	If you have no thought, no feelings at all for us, if you can let a perfect stranger walk into your life and take you away from us... we, who love you... if you can do that so easily, without considering the feelings for a single moment... what about your grandmother?

Pause.

CRISPIN: What about her? She's not going to miss me.

ALMA: Won't she? Won't she? How can you presume such a thing? Would you let her down? Betray her? That old lady who has always been so good, so kind to you? You were always her favourite, you know that. You know how much she loved you. There was never anything she wouldn't do for you. Why, I remember when you were only a baby...

JASON: We'd better split, baby.

ALMA: And now you turn against her.

CRISPIN: I haven't turned against anyone.

ALMA: You show her no respect at a time like this when it is needed the most. How do you think she will feel tomorrow? Knowing that the one she loved most has betrayed her, has played the Judas.

There is a long silence and then, slowly, CRISPIN walks towards the doors. For the first time the downstage door is opened and we see, beyond, a small anteroom in which stands a coffin. CRISPIN walks up to the coffin and stands beside it, looking down.

JASON: Don't bring me down, baby. Don't bring me down.

But there is no reaction from CRISPIN. JASON looks round the room at the women and nods his head slowly. Then he goes to the window and climbs out. ALMA follows, closes the windows and draws the curtains. She turns back into the room and the four women stand looking at Crispin as the curtain falls.

Other Titles Available

PLAYS

Are you Sitting Comfortably
Au Pair
Beautiful For Ever
Between Two Sighs
Early One Morning
Generations
Hear the Hyena Laugh
How do you Like your Wagner
Little Footsteps on the Petals
Oh Brother!
Red in the Morning
Rosemary
The 88
Third Drawer from the Top
Thriller of the Year
Twilight of Aunt Edna
Women Around

MUSICALS

Black Maria
Champagne Charlie
Cupid
Fugue In Two Flats
La Belle Otero
Peter Pan

For information on this
or any other available plays please contact:

info@dcgmediagroup.com   www.dcgmediagroup.com

www.ingramcontent.com/pod-product-compliance
Lightning Source LLC
Chambersburg PA
CBHW020013050426
42450CB00005B/451